20

Garden Layouts
to Die Digging For

Make a Beautiful Garden

Alecca Jackson

20 Garden Layouts to Die Digging For

Warning and Disclaimer

Every effort has been made to make this book as accurate as possible. However, no warranty or fitness is implied. The information provided is on an "as-is" basis. The author and the publisher shall have no liability or responsibility to any person or entity with respect to any loss or damages that arise from the information in this book.

Publisher Contact

Skinny Bottle Publishing
books@skinnybottle.com

Introduction

In this book, you will find design tips on what to plant, what furniture to use, and how to arrange things like walkways for myriad designs. This includes vegetable gardens and herb gardens, which will be covered in the two sections on vertical garden designs and container garden designs. This information will show you how to handle the process of designing and establishing your herb, fruit, or vegetable garden in different settings. The information learned applies to the other garden designs too, where it is noted that you can set up a small family garden with a patch for food, for example. However, for the sake of clarity and to avoid redundancy, this eBook will only go into the contents explicitly under the chapter "vegetable garden designs". The other chapters will give you tips on how to design family gardens with play areas, cottage gardens with their quintessential seating areas, as well as woodland gardens or rock gardens for those who live in harsher environments, wildflower gardens, even a small water garden. Chapters are dedicated to smaller versus larger designs and how to design things like Zen gardens in any sized space. You will not find a step by step blueprint, as there is a great deal of personalization that must go into each garden. It is up to you to decide which of the three recommended flowers you prefer to line the path to your reading nook, for example. That said, you will be given information necessary to incorporate the right structures, types of plants, water features, accessories, seating, and materials based on the design of your choosing. May it bring you peace throughout the process of designing and implementing your garden, and forever offer a tranquil place for relaxation.

Chapter One

Planning Your Garden

In this book, we will review the different garden designs available to you, some of the most popular. You will get an idea of what to include, what plants, colors, and furniture works best. However, a great garden does not happen overnight. You cannot just go to the store and fill your cart with some dirt, light fixtures, and plants. You have to carefully plan your garden.

So, sit down and start taking notes regarding your existing space.

Where do you see the sun fall during the day on your garden? At what times during the day, and during which seasons?

Before you make a blueprint for the design of your choosing, you need to take note of where and when sunlight hits your yard. This is important not just for plants, but if you want a sunbathing area along the side of a sheltered play area for kids, or a nice dining area sprinkled with shade during the evening hours.

How much privacy does your space afford and how much more, if any, do you want?

You might have neighbors who are somehow always curious and peering into your space. You might have an open yard with a property line that disappears at the end of that hill. In these cases, you will want to consider tall trees or a trellis to block the view and provide some privacy.

Will your garden require an outside tap?

If you do not already have a tap where you can connect a hose, then you might need one especially if you require irrigation for your yard. Having a tap can prove useful when kids bring home a wading pool or you want to set up a sprinkler system.

Next, you have to work out any practical matters.

Will your garden cater to a family? Do you want somewhere to read? Does it get frightening cold during the winter? Will you cater to pets? Are you going to host social events? Is the design a place to meditate?

Consider the needs of everyone who will be enjoying the space. If your dog loves running through flowerbeds, reconsider delicate flowers. If you have children, consider their safety. Water features without a basic may be, for example, better suited than a 2-foot deep pond for families with small children.

Finally, consider your storage needs. If you have patio furniture which is not weatherproof, make room for a storage shed. If you need a place for bikes or pool toys, also consider a storage shed. If you need a place for garden tools alone, look for seating that doubles as a storage unit underneath.

The design you choose needs to be made to fit the space you have, large or small. If your home boasts an incredible view, craft a space that opens up toward it. If you have nosy neighbors, form a boundary, a sense of privacy around the space so that you feel safe and enclosed. Create layers if you live on a hill. Add walkways, stairs, patios, and more to complement any existing structures or trees.

Creating the perfect garden is a combination of ambiance and foliage. Ambiance is what comes of your entire project. So, mix and match colors for plants, play around with the shape of your space, the lighting, and the accessories.

Borders

Regardless of which design you choose, your striking layout against with borders. Borders for the yard can take place in the form of a lawn, hedges, trees, even your favorite plants. The borders you create are formal and they define the different areas with precision and structure. They can also be informal if you prefer an emphasized arrangement of flowers. Informal settings are often mixed with more formal ideas today to create awe-inspiring designs.

When you are creating the exterior border to your garden space pay attention to the direction of your walls and any boundary fences you have. Consider where the sunlight will fit your yard naturally. Most of the greenery will grow along these areas. So, if you have a wall which faces east, most of your sunlight will happen in the early morning. If the walls of your yard face west, you will get the majority of your sunlight in the early and late afternoons. Walls facing south are very hot in the middle of the day and walls facing north only get about one hour of direct sunlight on a daily basis. If your walls face north then you should consider foliage that enjoy the shade and pay particular attention to the shade garden designs.

5

You should also consider the growing environment that your yard offers. If there is a plant that you absolutely love and must incorporate, then research what spot would be best for that plant. If you want to add vegetables or fruit you need to find a place that requires six hours of sun every day. If you live in an area that is windy you might want to clear your entire yard of any leads every week because otherwise, the wind will blow the seeds everywhere. Check the soil and are going to plant anything in your garden with a home-based soil test kit. These test kits help you to figure out if there's anything you have to add to the texture in order to cultivate the garden design you want. Some plants will not succeed in neutral soil or highly acidic soil. If you get readings from the soil kit and they indicate the pH level is above seven then the soil has high alkalinity. Anything below seven is highly acidic. You can certainly find plants that fit either soil but if, again, there's something you absolutely love and want to have in your design, you might have to add something to the soil to make it a more hospitable environment.

This is particularly true if you are planting something as your border. Low growing plants provide great ground cover and they work by softening any paved area in your garden. You can plant some taller plants if you want to plant them as low groups. Rounded plants are great if you want to display contrast or if you need to fill extra space in a plant bed. Baby's breath and lavender shrubs are perfect examples of this. Spiked plants like yucca or cabbage tree create a nice dome shaped and are very eye-catching. Of course, fruits and vegetables will transform any design and provide you with tasty treats. We will cover more information on planting fruits, vegetables, and herbs later on.

Accessories

There are many accessories that you can choose for your garden, regardless of the design you consider. Items like birdhouses, statues, and bird baths are available in nearly limitless styles and designs. They make excellent additions to any of the garden designs listed in this book. These items should be the final pieces that you add to your design so be sure to choose carefully. Statues are very popular for more upscale gardens. Ancient royalty would have the likeness of heroes or gods in their gardens and today that's still a time-honored tradition. If you decide to include a pond in your garden you might want to add a metal statue of men holding fishing poles, or different animals. Abstract artwork can be fun especially if you have a local metal shop nearby where conversation pieces are purchased at a reasonable fee. Whatever you add to your private haven make sure that you are comfortable with it. Just because there are a dozen garden gnomes on sale does not mean that they should be final accessories to your garden. You are the one who will have to live in this relaxing space so choose carefully.

Outdoor Rooms

For a more formal garden space, you might prefer an outdoor room that is fully enclosed and has its own electrical system for seating, air-conditioning, and lighting. This is a slightly more expensive but obviously more formal alternative to an open deck, pergola, or gazebo.

Outdoor rooms are a great way to create a unique hideaway inside of your garden. With the most basic outdoor room, you get protection from unpredictable weather. You can create a semi-enclosed or fully enclosed space in which to serve drinks for relaxing. Outdoor rooms do not have to be complex. The basic G box structure will meet most garden needs. You get a variety of door and window options and these rooms are prewired electrically. The cost for a room that is complete is roughly $45,000. Inside a space like this, you can create a sauna full of natural light or a greenhouse. If you on your property an outdoor room like this will not only enhance your garden but add to your property value. If you choose to install an outdoor room you must be cognizant of where you plan to place it as it will remain a permanent structure. Conversely, there are temporary structures that you can move around from time to time if you choose to alter your focal point throughout the year. There are some outdoor rooms that come with EC smart glass which is a glaze that changes from clear glass to a black glass in order to improve any UV protection and reduce glare. Still, there are low maintenance outdoor rooms which have eco-friendly glass rooms that keep the costs for heating and cooling the interior structure very low.

That said, it is time to look at the many different layouts available to you for your garden design.

Chapter Two

Social Garden Design

For those who enjoy entertaining guests, a social garden design is ideal. This design takes into consideration privacy above all else. The best way to provide such privacy not only for yourself, your family, and your guests, is to plant trees and plants called "climbers" to form a natural screen. If you opt for trees, be sure to avoid planting them too close to your home or that of any neighbor because the roots can, with time, damage your foundation. You can, alternatively, place trees at the end of the garden area to form a screen which does not hinder the view you have from your home.

Once you have established your privacy, you need to create a seating area. You might consider a deck and built in future. This can be very sleek, customized to your garden theme or tastes, and is typically weatherproof. Weatherproof furniture is an important component. If you are going to build a deck and add outdoor furniture to this design, you want to measure the amount of shade and sunlight your garden area receives. You will have to keep track of where the sun falls throughout the day and where the warmth will be. When dining, for example, people tend to prefer shade. If your yard is sunny most of the time with no naturally shaded area, you will need to plant something that creates shade, like a row of tall bushes which form a screen. Under this screen, you can place your outdoor dining furniture.

If you intend to mingle outside with your guests, avoid laying down grass and leaving the garden as is. Instead, plant colorful flowers which attract bees or butterflies. Lavender, for example, will bring many buzzing friends to your dinner parties. Plant climbers such as clematis armandii add a bit of architectural flair, as will spiky plants like palms.

Be practical about the design. If you want to include a dining area, for example, you might not have room to include a garden shed. This means that your gardening tools will need a new home. In such cases, try to think practically: use seats or design a table that has a lid on top and doubles as a tabletop workbench. This allows you a place to store your garden tools discreetly while you are entertaining.

When it comes to seating look for comfort no matter the design you want. Invest money in seat cushions which are weatherproof. Guests will want someplace soft to sit and relax when you bring them outside. Investing in seat cushions means extending the longevity of your outdoor furniture but can easily be thrown in the wash if they get too dirty.

If you decide to have an outdoor deck, one that is raised, you will need to visually soften the edges. This does not mean you have to change the outdoor deck design, but rather, leave the deck protruding and cover the borders with different plants. The best plans to use our scented herbs or fresh herbs because they will not only visually soften the social garden design, they smell great, and if you are cooking outside and simply pick one or two fresh herbs to sprinkle on top of your dishes.

As a finishing touch to your social garden design, consider adding trellises around your dining area. Trellises offer a very coordinated and neat appearance. They are also easier amended than old fences. Perhaps best of all is the fact that you can train scented climbing plants to grow up the trellis like Jasmine. This not only gives you a private escape that is aesthetically appealing but offers a wonderful aroma.

Walkways Increase Accessibility

Adding a walkway to the garden design offers multiple advantages. First and perhaps most obvious is your garden becomes more accessible. Second, you increase your ability to move around from one place to the next without stumbling upon uneven ground or tripping over a delicate flower. For social garden designs, you will have many guests traipsing around your garden and if you have

13

walkways you can insist that all guests stick to the walkway so that they do not harm any of your vulnerable, valuable, or rare plants. You can protect your garden investments while still granting your guests access to your design.

Another benefit to walkways, especially a wooden walkway, is the wheelchair accessibility. If you have a friend or family member who is confined to a wheelchair, you can make a wonderful and memorable evening out by offering them the chance to enjoy your garden.

Patios

For your social garden design, if you are hosting outdoor cookouts for parties you might consider incorporating the patio for additional accessibility and functionality. Figure out what you want the patio to be used for and that will help you figure out the size. A small space which is roughly 8' x 8' is perfect if you just want to cook but not necessarily seat all of your guests on the patio. There are many shapes available including rectangular and square shapes for attractive patio designs. Squares are obviously the more traditional route.

If you create your small patio you can use bricks, tiles, or landscaping stones or the design. This is perfect if you plan on having any type of seating area and need a level surface on which to place your furniture. If you already have a patio you can accent the area with a pergola or a gazebo.

With regard to the materials available for your patio, concrete is durable and easily customizable. You can change the color before you mix the concrete but it can only be poured in good weather and

14

can be expensive. Paving stones are a more attractive option that is reasonably priced but in order for you to use paving stones, you have to prepare the area by making it level. Brick is great because of the starting performance and variety of color options. The only downside with brick is that the site, much like with paving stones, have to be prepared ahead of time so that each brick fit snugly with those bricks around it. Gravel is the final choice available in multiple sizes, styles, and colors. It's very affordable but if your patio is being used for dining, gravel will provide a sturdy surface for your furniture.

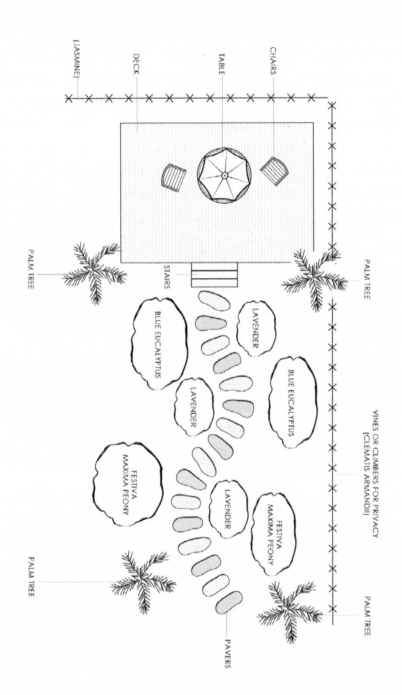

SOCIAL GARDEN

Chapter Three

Small City Garden Design

For those of you who live in a city and have a very small space, do not fret. You can make a small city garden that provides you with utility, privacy, and feels much bigger than it is.

The design for a small city garden has to be very well organized so that it delivers not only the degree of privacy that a city dweller will need, ample seating opportunities for guests but structural plants and style. The result will be a space that truly encapsulates a vibrant energy in which you can relax after a long day in the city.

Seating is one of the most important considerations for a small city garden design. The most significant feature you will find in any small garden is a very attractive table and a matching bench set. The reason for this is quite simple. That piece of furniture becomes the focal point. So it doubles as a structural device and a place for seating. As such it is important to make sure it is as attractive as possible.

17

Beyond the seating, you can create a great screen with role bamboo trees or all of the trees. This not only creates a strong structural presence in your garden but it acts as a boundary. The repetition created by a row of trees seamlessly blending into the rest of your garden creates a sense of harmony.

You will need a small footpath more than likely from your back door or side door to the seating area in the garden. Along this path, you should have low plants. These low plants will help offset a bigger paved region that a city garden usually has and it brings the green color much closer to the area of the garden you will use the most. If you don't have room for a large lawn or you simply cannot care for one, you can try a low maintenance gravel surface. This will also give you a space for extra seating opportunities. If you feel so inclined you can blend paving stones with different granite chips to add some variety in this space in lieu of a traditional lawn.

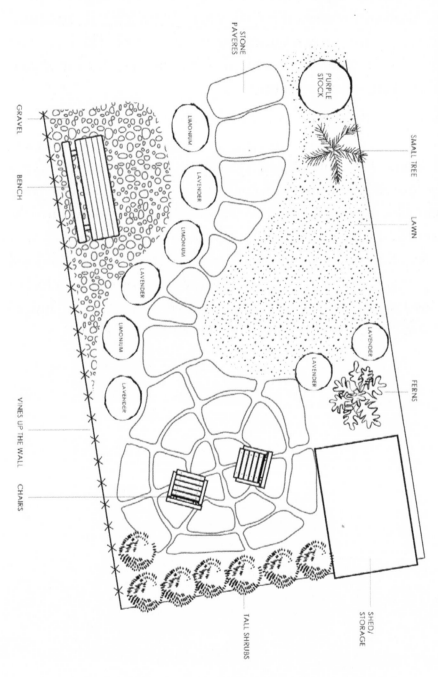

SMALL CITY GARDEN

STONE PAVERES

PURPLE STOCK

SMALL TREE

LAWN

LIMONIUM

LAVENDER

LIMONIUM

GRAVEL

BENCH

LAVENDER

LIMONIUM

LAVENDER

LAVENDER

LAVENDER

FERNS

VINES UP THE WALL

CHAIRS

SHED/ STORAGE

TALL SHRUBS

Chapter Four

Sloping Garden Design

Not everybody has a flat square or rectangular space in which to design their garden. Many people who live in very distinct regions around the world will have a sloping yard space which means the garden designs get slightly trickier. If you have a sloping garden space you have to use hard landscaping and different levels. The biggest challenge that you will likely face is finding a suitable theme and plants to match.

The best way to start this design is to divide the greenery into many spaces along your slope which creates levels. You can even use terraces to create different levels. As you work your way up or down the slope you might even consider making one level a dining region where you will find a beautiful set of tables and chairs to catch the last of the setting sun, and then leave one of the other levels for a row brightly colored flowers or a small pond and water fixture. You have the freedom to make each level distinct with its unique aesthetic flavor. One of the ways to plants many different items in such a limited space to use clipped boxes. These boxes will look neat

21

in their appearance and they will echo the strong lines that you have to establish with a sloping garden design.

Sloped gardens naturally draw the eye to the end and the top. For that reason, you want to make sure that whatever you have at the top end of your garden makes an impression. This might be a small bench beneath a tree, a unique garden sculpture, or an aesthetically designed set of tables and chairs.

When you have a sloping garden you can add plants which have unique shapes to them like spiky grasses, box hedges, herbs, or lettuces. This will draw the attention from the shape of the garden and focus instead on the many garden sections you have designed. Container gardening is a suitable alternative for this and if you use containers, be sure to utilize one material and one color for your pots to heighten the neatness of the design.

Once you create different levels, make sure to designate each level with a purpose. Zone one of the terraced garden might be set aside for dining with some to set aside for reading on a bench, and zone three designated for container vegetables and herbs.

The final touches for a sloping garden design are the steps. Your steps have to be practical above all else. You all can naturally mix-and-match the materials you use to make the steps a more attractive component. However, make sure that whatever material you choose is something that you can walk on if it is wet.

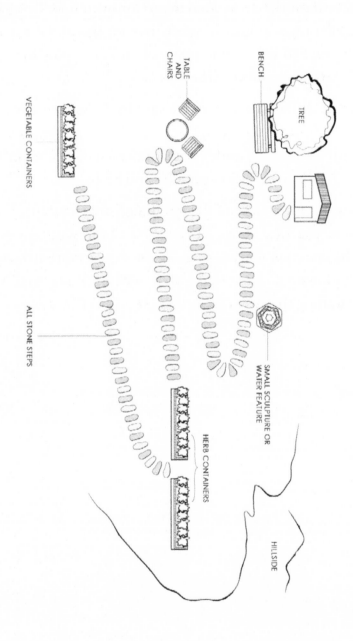

SLOPING GARDEN

BENCH

TREE

TABLE
AND
CHAIRS

VEGETABLE CONTAINERS

ALL STONE STEPS

SMALL SCULPTURE OR
WATER FEATURE

HERB CONTAINERS

HILLSIDE

Chapter Five

Rooftop Garden Design

If you have a rooftop garden space that you want to turn it into a verdant entertainment and relaxation space, consider that hidden rooftop gardens are a wonderful way to reconnect with nature as an urban resident. However, the soil that you bring it to your rooftop garden design will be restricted to containers. The plants and garden foliage are subject to unrelenting sun in most cases and wind exposure that plants do not otherwise get at the ground level. As such, your two biggest battles will be maintaining the right water levels and preventing desiccation.

The rooftop garden can still be converted into the perfect escape by grouping the plants together so that they are not only green and vibrant but they can better fight off the impact of negative weather. The use of vertical planting with tall plants and trees in containers is best for surrounding your lateral views and the views of any overlooking the neighboring rooftops. These trees by extension not only create privacy but provide you with physical shelter from the wind.

25

On the note of shelter is best for you to design your seating area deliberately located in the parts of your rooftop garden that gets the highest amount of shelter from the wind. You might want to put your seats right next to the containers especially if you have packed your containers full of delightfully scented herbs like rosemary or lavender. This will give guests the impression that your small getaway is far away from the city it overlooks.

Every plant you put on your rooftop garden needs to be placed in a container that you can cluster the containers together to create a boundary or order. One of the best things about container planting is that you have the freedom to move the pots around until you find a combination that you are best, without causing any damage to the growing plants. Another advantage is that you don't have to water groups of container plants as often as you do standalone plants. The plants naturally create a shelter against drought.

As part of this design, you can install a timber deck that is a flexible open space and breaks up the composition of the space. Timber decks are lighter and more practical installed or concrete which is why they are best on a rooftop.

ROOFTOP GARDEN

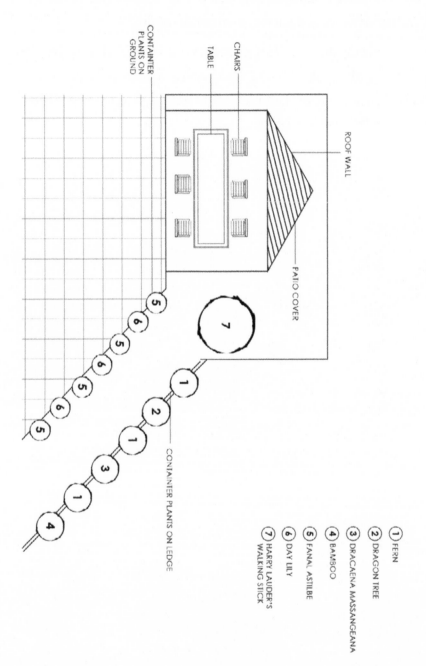

CONTAINER PLANTS ON GROUND

TABLE

CHAIRS

ROOF WALL

PATIO COVER

CONTAINER PLANTS ON LEDGE

1. FERN
2. DRAGON TREE
3. DRACAENA MASSANGEANA
4. BAMBOO
5. FANAL ASTILBE
6. DAY LILY
7. HARRY LAUDER'S WALKING STICK

28

Chapter Six

Low-Maintenance Garden Design

While of course, it would be great to have a garden design that requires absolutely no maintenance on your behalf, there is no such thing. What you can do is set up a low maintenance garden. The key to this is to create something interesting in its ambiance and appealing to your friends and family without adding plants or shrubs that are difficult to care for. Hard landscaping, in particular, is one way to add interest using various materials and limit the amount of space where plants are required. Picking plants that you only have to prune once a month is best.

When establishing this garden design you need to divide your space. This is important. If you are, for example, not going to use your backyard space for a small soccer field, then you can divide it into similarly sized rectangular sections or square sections. When things are divided it is easier to make smaller spaces inside of which you have simple designs. With multiple spaces, you can change the materials you use and alter the colors ever so slightly. You can add things like herbs or small flowers to soften the division between each section. You can even add shade and color and change the height of your garden by introducing tall translucent plants.

One example is the verbena which is not only a great color but it will come back year after year. If you prefer something with a similar shape but more permanent, consider bamboo. If you plant bamboo you have to plant inside containers sunk into your flower bed. If you overlook this crucial step your bamboo shoots will start appearing in your gravel or anywhere in your separate garden spaces that you don't want it to be like in between paving stones.

If you want to infuse some life into low maintenance garden design the best way to spruce it up is to add some color. Color can be derived from masonry, hard landscaping, even a small and circularly paved seating area that utilizes bright tiles. Adding color does not mean you have to cover the entire space with flowers. If you want to create a more traditional symbol space you can add greens, pale blues, and cream colors. If you prefer a contemporary look then try to find colors which contrast the natural surroundings which means red, purple, gray, even black. If you are unsure what color you want for your furniture for your tiles you can always take a swatch of that color and compare it to the garden space to see what works and what doesn't.

In a low maintenance garden design sculpture and shape is very important. You can, for example, plant hedges in blocks for Rose and lead space in between four paving stones. This is a wonderful way to add some interest without adding to your workload. If you buy young plants you will have the freedom to shape them however you want which doesn't need to be done frequently, so it won't add to your garden maintenance, and it saves you money because younger plants are less expensive. In fact, if you set up plants for your hedge you only need to trim them twice a year. One great trip for a garden like this is to plant a variety of heights. Plant each of your items separately but then mix and match the ground cover plants with different trees.

For a low maintenance garden design, if you want to include a garden path you want something that looks great all year round. This is a grass path. You can divvy up your lawn into small sections and keep the spaces of the squares the width of your lawnmower. Then plant decorative grasses into that square. Each of the squares will be finished off with a nice lawn edging. You can, for contrast, but large black pebbles on your path instead and surround the large black pebbles with white gravel. This will show off different brightly colored plants in a stylish fashion. Of course, you can always plant something like the beautifully purple flax flowers around your walking path or something ornamental like black grass.

For a low maintenance space, you want low maintenance plants. You certainly don't want to spend all your time pruning and cutting. So, if you are going to plant trees, consider the Amur Maple tree. This tree will eventually reach a peak of 20-30 feet and is quite versatile. You will need to prune it a bit if you buy a young tree, but once it starts to branch out it will start growing dense groups of trunks which are all near one another. The tree takes on a naturally round shape with dense foliage. All of this gives you a lot of shade.

If you want a big, blooming fruit tree for the summer, the Crabapple Tree will reach a height around 20 feet and a large width. These trees flourish in sunny areas, so if your garden is already heavily shaded, you should consider another tree. Also note that since this is a fruit tree, once a year it will start to drop its fruit and your garden area will be covered in said fruit. So, if you do not want to clean up this mess, consider another tree.

One of the more popular trees in America is the Flowering Dogwood. This tree has beautiful white blooms and will add a lot of "oooh" and "aww" to any social event. The trees reach between 20-35 feet at maturity and require very little maintenance.

Native to North America is the Southern Hawthorne tree, one which offers gorgeous foliage all year round. There are white blooms which eventually are replaced by bright red or orange fruit that stays all winter long.

The Japanese Magnolia is another great tree, but it does not have any big color change to wow your guests. The leaves are wide and dense. At maturity, the trees can be as wide as they are tall, and their lower branches can touch the ground. You might not have to worry about this at the start of your garden, but decades later, it could be an issue.

LOW MAINTENANCE

① PURPLE FLAX FLOWERS

② ORNAMENTAL BLACK GRASS

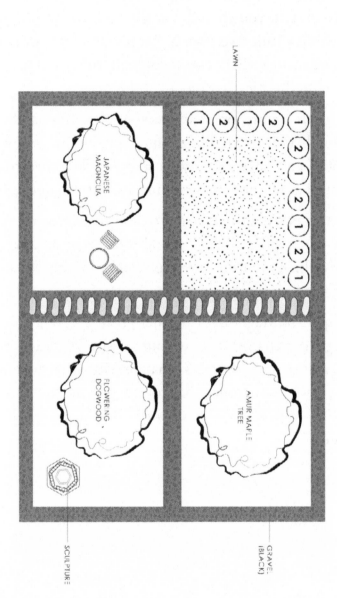

LAWN

PAVING STONES (WHITE)

JAPANESE MAGNOLIA

FLOWERING DOGWOOD

AMUR MAPLE TREE

SCULPTURE

GRAVEL (BLACK)

34

Chapter Seven

Contemporary Garden Design

For contemporary Garden designs, you want something that is elegant in its style but also practical with a high-end design. The garden itself needs to cater to your needs. This means it should provide a restful place for relaxation, create shade to block out harsh summer light, and perhaps even be a source of food by way of the vegetables and herbs you plant.

If you have children or you want to entertain in this garden you need to have a deck. The deck is a practical place for dining, playing, and lounging. Once your deck is installed is very low maintenance. If you have a lawn which grows to the edge of the deck, you can divide the two areas and soften that division with low plants. Add colorful foliage and easy to care for plants like blue flax.

If your garden happens to overlook a rather unsightly view such as an adjacent cemetery, on camps neighboring home, or anything else, you can create a screen using tall plants. If your garden happens to run the back of a noisy footpath place these tall plants along the border to help deaden the noise. The best plans for this are ones

35

which will not outgrow the garden space but will still fulfill their purpose. Cordylines or bamboos are best.

If the garden space is busy, define it with graphic patterns. Graphic patterns make your garden feel cleaner and neater. Consider using square slabs set in gravel and lined with small flowers to help soften each of your borders. This is quite easy to manage and will add some visual interest to the elegant design.

Next, you want to create your lounge space. Whether you want to lounge out in the sun or in the shade you will have to start by setting up a hard surface on which to place your outdoor furniture. If you put your lounge table and chairs on the grass it will slowly sink into the grass and eventually sit unevenly causing the graph below to die. If you already have an area that provides natural shade, use it. This is a great bonus that many gardens do not have. If you have a region in your yard which is partially shaded, that is truly the best because you won't have to move chairs around as the day goes on.

You can avoid having to trim the different garden paths by edging the borders of your garden. Use mulch on these borders. Mulch will maintain the cleanliness of the plants and protect them from cold and sun exposure. Mulch will also maintain moisture in your soil and prevent the growth of weeds. You will greatly reduce the amount of work you have to put into tending to your garden by using mulch.

You can select low maintenance plants with a variety of scents, leaf shapes, and colors. Be sure to pick plants that prefer shade for your border spots that might never see the sun, and plants that love sun for the sunny regions in your garden.

Creating a small footpath using slabs of wood or rocks can help prevent your elegant design from being trodden down. If you have trees already in your yard that you have been dying to get rid of, consider shopping them down believing their stump and roots in place. This can be converted into a natural step over for a pond or small stream that you build into your design.

Having a walkway through your garden helps to not only provide access but to create the layout you desire. When you select the materials for your garden walkway you need to take into consideration the past you prefer. Exotic hardwoods are more durable than softwood like pine. You can also find hardwood options that have beautiful color patterns and unique grain. Another viable option though costly is composite decking. Obviously, the material you select will become an integral component of your garden so choose wisely.

In addition to regular walkways that take people from one main area of the garden to another, you might want smaller garden paths. When you are creating your garden paths be sure to play around with scale. You might consider using giant, round pebbles for the pathway to your lawn. Alternatively, you might prefer a straight and long path with large pebbles that snake through the long path. All of these materials can be purchased at any garden or landscape center.

For a garden design like this do not let the walkways become boring. Add angles and create angular pathways that bring the eye to some of the more detailed components to your garden. If you have flowerbeds that you are quite proud of, try a zigzag shape that works its way around the flower beds so that anyone visiting has to walk around your artwork. Order the paths with stone or wood which will stand in sharp contrast to pebble walkways. If you prefer a natural path consider bark chips. One of the nice things about detailing your flowerbeds with these geometrically designed paths is that you can reach all of your flowerbeds when you need to tend to them or water them without damaging any other part of your garden.

You might consider using a seasonal design. If, for example, you plan to use this garden primarily in the spring and summer to sit outside and read with a glass of iced tea, plant a swath of things like blue tulips that snake around your walking path and a seating area so that you can walk out to your reading nook along a riverbed of blue tulips.

And of course, don't forget to use your senses. Put plants along your path which release a fragrant scent as you walk by. Accidentally brushing some of the plants with your leg will add a heightened sense, literally, to your garden if you have planted rosemary bushes or lavender along the route.

CONTEMPORARY GARDEN

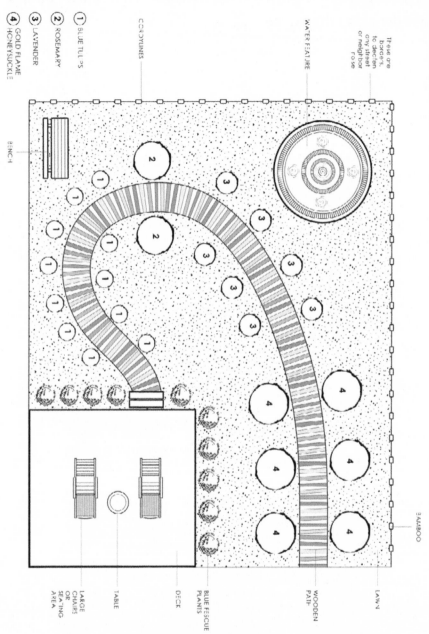

① BLUE TULIPS

② ROSEMARY

③ LAVENDER

④ GOLD FLAME HONEYSUCKLE

CORDYLINES

WATER FEATURE

These are borders, to declen any street or neighbor rose

BENCH

BAMBOO

LAWN

WOODEN PATH

BLUE FESCUE PLANTS

DECK

TABLE

LARGE CHAIRS OR SEATING AREA

Chapter Eight

Urban City Garden Design

There are many unique shapes and sizes for urban city Garden designs. The most common design shape is the L shape. This shape is challenging because the view from the side is often bland and the space might be too small to support a deck or another outdoor room. As such your first step when working with a garden design like this is to define the spaces. Your goal in all of this should be to create a garden which in spite of its small size is full of interest. Planting is typically the most obvious solution but plants take up a lot of room and you should only plant items which are architectural showpieces.

This leaves you with options like hard landscaping. Known as hard escaping, you can change the hard materials you use to create a quiet space, hidden from view, protected from the elements, with adequate seating. Remember that no garden design is complete without some form of seating. If you have an awkwardly shaped garden space you can add a half wall that hugs the seating area or an outdoor bench.

For urban designs, keep it simple but try to make the most out of the space. Play around with the angles you have to add a great amount of detail. Try putting in a deck that runs in one direction and add lines from your pay. The run in the opposite direction. Your eye will be naturally drawn to these lines which can play a visual trip on your guests and create the impression that the physical space is much larger than it is.

You can even hang plants out of your windows to make the most of bright flowers you love, herbs you cook with, etc.

Because the space you have is limited, you only want to plant items that will grow all year round. You can use a row of shrubs or small trees in bright colors to break up the landscape of your garden. If you have a fanse you can always paint or stain in a bright color. White fences will make the garden spacing bigger and brightly colored fences will show off the garden furniture or stand in stark contrast to the plans you have. For a more modern look, somber gray tones will add contrast.

If you need seating in your garden design, do some homework before you buy. Picking furniture for your garden design is not as easy as it seems. There are so many styles and materials from which to choose.

Wicker furniture is some of the oldest furniture styles we know. In fact, there are references to wicker furniture being used by the ancient Egyptians. This is a popular choice today because you can get it with a white paint coating or you can get it in an unfinished design. Wicker is popular for its comfort. Oversized chairs and couches can be padded with large pillows making your outdoor space ideal for relaxation and reading.

Wrought iron is often found in high traffic areas because of its durability. Today you can find wrought iron pieces that are actually made of steel. Many homeowners prefer wrought iron as it ties in with metal statues or fences. One of the only issues with this is that damp weather will result in rust. You can treat your furniture with Rust-O-Leum in a handful of colors.

If you prefer, there are exotic hardwoods you can use for your outdoor furniture, like Ipe or Tiger Wood, which are known for their beautiful colors, durability, and hardness. Rich color tones stand in high contrast to natural plants and foliage, which makes these woods so popular. Softer woods like fir or pine cannot withstand bad weather and you will need to get a water seal on them or bring them inside before it rains.

Plastic is another alternative, one which is much less expensive. Plastic can be purchased in a variety of colors and is easy to clean. You do not have to worry about water damage, but you should not leave plastic furniture in the sun or it will start to fade.

Once you have picked the material, look at the size of your garden to figure out whether you prefer/have space for swings, gliders, chairs, or loveseats. If you are entertaining primarily, you will need to capitalize on as much seating as you can get.

URBAN CITY LAYOUT

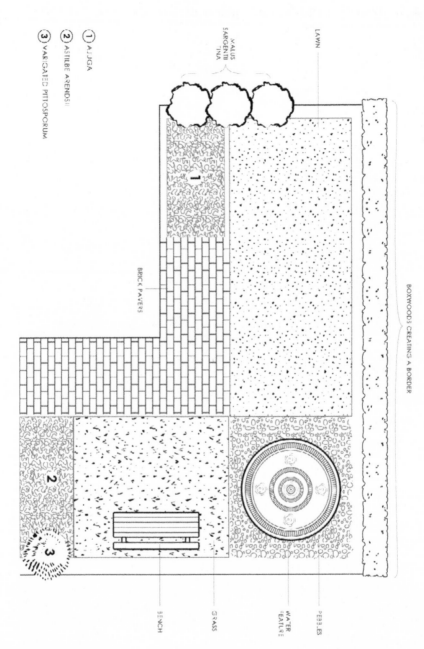

① AJUGA
② ASTILBE ARENDSII
③ VARIEGATED PITTOSPORUM

MALUS SARGENTII 'TINA'

LAWN

BRICK PAVERS

BOXWOODS CREATING A BORDER

BENCH

GRASS

WATER FEATURE

PEBBLES

46

Chapter Nine

Family Garden Design

Family gardens do so much more than grow a handful of flowers. They are a terrific place to encourage social activities, give children a space to run around, and even encourage their imagination. If done correctly, such a friendly design will encourage people to come outside and sit for hours.

For a family garden, you should have a patio region that gives solid footing for tables and chairs with a view of the entire yard. This is important as a parent. You need to make sure you can have eyes on your kids at all times. Consider a lawn where children can play. The lawn should be small enough to be resodded if it gets worn out and provide a break from all of your other plants or structures. The lawn can be a place for games like soccer, catch, badminton, etc.... Keep a container for storage outside where sports equipment and games can be held. Then, when kids are done with their homework, they can go find the games they want to play without parental supervision.

A small circular walkway can offer you a transitional point from things like planter beds to your lawn. If you can afford the space, including play area bordered by something like sunken logs so that the kids can hop on the logs or sit on them. The triangular sandbox is our great for younger kids. Tried to also include a vegetable garden separated from your play area by a low fence. Make sure your vegetable garden is protected from any pets you have. This garden can bring the family together and offer healthy foods.

When kids are learning how to ride a bike they love unbroken stretch of concrete. When kids are young sidewalk out front will work just fine. So don't rush to replace your front sidewalk with flagstones. A circular cement walkway around the perimeter of your backyard. Your kids a racetrack for their toys and scooters.

When you look out at your space, think about where you want to draw social gatherings. Comfortable seating and tables draw your family into your garden when the weather is nice. If you have a large tree, it might be best to set up your tables and chairs underneath it so that you can benefit from the shade. Otherwise, a large umbrella might offer shade and protection from rain if you need it. If you create a deck it will be easy for you to clean it. This is something to consider when you have little ones running around. In addition to this think of the table and chairs as a place for not just dining but playing board games, doing arts and crafts, even arranging bouquets of flowers. A small seating area like this will give your family a chance to leave the house without having to drive anywhere.

Create a space where kids can imaginations run wild. Sandboxes, simple sandboxes are of creative think tanks for children. You can put the sandbox on top of your lawn, build it into the ground so that it is level with the lawn. Some people prefer building a sandbox right next to the outdoor dining tables so that kids and adults can work and play in close proximity to one another. When kids start to outgrow the sandbox, think about water. Get rid of that stand and convert the sunken spot with waterproof liners so the kids now have a small wading pool. It might even later become a water garden or a fish pond where family fish can be kept in a loving environment.

A wooden area that has something to climb, slide, even a swing is perfect for kids. You can purchase the structures premade so that you just fit all the main components together. You can also build your own individual structures so that you have exactly what fits into the space provided. A basketball hoop, if you have the space for it, can be set up in one distinct part of the yard for a quick game of pickup or conversely, a paved roller skate hockey game. Take into consideration what activities your kids currently enjoy and what things you plan to do as a family before you allocate space for certain things.

Everybody thinks of the quintessential treehouse is the perfect escape that there are other things you can do to set up a private area for games like hide and seek, tea parties, for sleepovers. Eight tepees can be made out of bamboo canes, a small outdoor room can be set up inside large bushes so that it appears covered like a secret fort. Set the stage, literally. If you build a secret fort that is on the ground level, or you have a patio or deck, consider allocating a part of the space as a state, a place for kids to perform. Kids are always finding new ways to turn old objects into something protect. You can set up a small box outside where kids can store their play items or the constant and then, during the summer months, adults can sit on the patio furniture and watch as the kids put on a show.

Make room in an existing storage shed for a small kid-sized table where tea parties can be held, mud pies can be made, and child-sized watering cans can be found. Kids love to help water things so let them have at it, so to speak. If you have the space for it, have your kids help you design a small vegetable or herb garden. Let them play a role in picking out what sweet treats to plant, like strawberries, sugar snap peas, or cherry tomatoes. Then they have healthy snacks they can pick themselves while they play. With the family garden, the types of flowers or trees you include are not nearly as important as providing a space for kids to get dirty, play with pets, water things, and enjoy make-believe.

FAMILY GARDEN

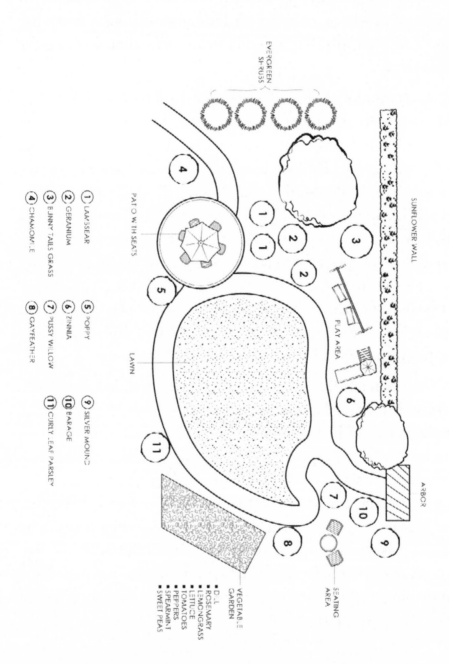

EVERGREEN
SHRUBS

SUNFLOWER WALL

PATIO WITH SEATS

PLAY AREA

LAWN

ARBOR

SEATING
AREA

① LAMB'SEAR
② GERANIUM
③ BUNNY TAILS GRASS
④ CHAMOMILE

⑤ POPPY
⑥ ZINNIA
⑦ PUSSY WILLOW
⑧ GAYFEATHER

⑨ SILVER MOUND
⑩ BARAGE
⑪ CURLY LEAF PARSLEY

VEGETABLE
GARDEN

■ DILL
■ ROSEMARY
■ LEMONGRASS
■ LETTUCE
■ TOMATOES
■ PEPPERS
■ SPEARMINT
■ SWEET PEAS

52

Chapter Ten

Cottage Garden Design

Cottage gardens do not look like they were designed. Usually, they have freely growing flowers and exuberant deal. In order to achieve this informal look with formal planning do not plant anything in a straight line with the defined pattern. You want your plants to cascade over your walking paths and weave into one another. This adds to the charm. Moreover, if you add self-seeding plants that will eventually start popping up in unexpected places which only adds to the exuberant feel. Cottage gardens are usually filled with the same traditional plants and flowers that your grandmother would have grown. Foxglove, columbine, pansy, snapdragon, bleeding heart, bachelor's button, and Cosmos are among old-fashioned flowers that you should consider.

When you plan for your furniture, you want to add comfortable furniture. You can convert cottage garden design into an outdoor living space by avoiding anything contemporary. Search instead for painted metal shellback chairs for wicker furniture. More importantly, your furniture doesn't have to match. Part of the charm of cottage garden design is the informality and the eclectic mixture. Look for Romantic plants that are soft to the touch. Many cottage gardens have a rather romantic feel, slightly whimsical. Part of that is actually the result of the flowers. Many people plant blooms which offer soft, pastel shades. You also want plants that are packed with petals like old roses. More fragrant varieties are better.

When it comes to the materials you use, include structures which are made from natural materials that would or otherwise well-worn materials. Weathered wood fences, gates, and arborist will fit right in with the collection of cottage plants. If you can't find something which has a weathered look to it, you can build a brand-new structure will purchase a brand-new structure and then send it down to give it the appearance without altering the composition.

If you set up a pathway, to ensure that it does not follow a straight or structured line. Always create a soft, meandering path. Paving materials like wood chips, old bricks, flagstone, all work very long cottage garden designs. If you are going to accessorize, add vintage old antique items. You can look through garage sales to find the perfect accessory instead of purchasing high ticket accessories. Things like old, dented watering cans or dates that have peeling paint will work well. Certainly do not be afraid of a creative use for an outdated item. That old, dented watering that might not work well and may be covered in a bit of rust, can easily be converted into a planter box. An old chicken feeder can now be used as another planter box. Your rusty trowel can be a new gate handle.

If you can, try to incorporate a white picket fence. Not every cottage garden has one but they tend to be paired if possible. You don't necessarily have to use it to make a boundary but, you can include just a short section of it even as a trellis that holds up your favorite perennials. Overall, incorporate elements that you love. Don't get caught up trying to force informal look. Plant things that you like and make sure that the garden suits you. And of course, tucked away somewhere at the end of the winding path surrounded by old-fashioned flowers should be a table and chair that beckons visitors to take a moment to sit down and appreciate all that you have done.

COTTAGE GARDEN

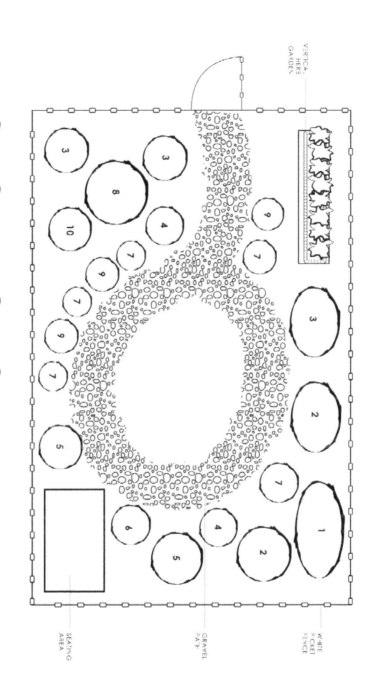

(1) PEAS

(2) PHLOX

(3) ASTERS

(4) HOLLYHOCKS

(5) PURPLE CONEFLOWER

(6) COSMOS

(7) DAISIES

(8) ZINNIAS

(9) VIOLETS

(10) SNAPDRAGON

VERTICAL HERB GARDEN

SEATING AREA

GRAVEL PATH

WHITE PICKET FENCE

57

Chapter Eleven

Rock Garden Design

If you live in a region that is high in altitude, located in the mountains, the garden design you choose will have to stand up to the harsh conditions that high-altitude brings with it such as high winds, drought, and intense sun. Rock garden designs are a wonderful option in such settings because they contain plants which grow naturally on high mountains. You should experiment with different wildflowers. If you want a layered look which is more monochromatic, combine groundcover with differently sized shrubs to provide a vertical interest.

You don't have to have a rocky garden already to create a rock garden design. Even if you don't live high in the mountains you can create this design in your yard. Put up a stone wall as a foundation and border for low growing alpine plants like Potentilla, Aubrieta "Royal Blue". Then, fill in the tiny crevices between stones to give more color to the stone wall with Dianthus "Tiny Rubies" or Gypsophila franzii.

To maximize the visual interest here, play around with the texture and change the scale of the rocks and plants. Mix perennials, shrubs, and conifers to blend colorful blooms with distinct foliage. Create a winding path with bricks if you need a place to walk. If you have a dry creek bed on your property, fill it with Mexican pebbles.

Should you have a sloping space, you can still do a rock garden design by bringing in locally sourced boulders and plants. Combine creeping cedar, Japanese maples, cannas, pines, yucca, and ornamental grasses to make a grand display. This will make your yard vibrant and perhaps best of all, alleviate any need to ever mow another lawn.

As you integrate flowers, think of eye-catching colors like bright orange blossoms from Eriogonum umbellatum, which will be great against an otherwise bland backdrop. Conversely, plant some Mojave sage and enjoy its pink blooms. Both of these plants will thrive with next to no maintenance and they are drought tolerant.

If you want your rock garden to bloom year-round, then evergreens should be planted too. These can keep some color inside your design when the warm yellow, pink, and red blooms of the desert plants fade away.

Add groundcover around the rocks. For groundcover, you can plant things with blue or purple hues like the aforementioned Aubrieta "Royal Blue" or Veronic "waterperry blue". Try Saxifraga if you want something small with pink blooms. Or, you can plant groundcover in the form of feathery foliage. Low growing junipers are the best because they are an evergreen, they will fill in space between your rocks fast, they tolerate droughts, and they will offset the bright colors of the flowers you plant. When you are working with a rock garden design, you should consider color and form together. Pair dwarf conifers with your favorite perennials to that you add more height and texture to your garden. This will help your bright pink floral blooms stand out against the sculptural form of the boulders and dwarf conifers. When you plant the conifers, plant them behind or next to other low-growers so that there is still visual balance in your yard. You can blend drifts of thyme, oregano, sedum, and yarrow together and watch as they start to grow into one another, casually spilling onto your brick walkway.

Drought tolerant plants and rocks are natural neighbors, do not worry. Neither require a lot of care and will look lush without any extra watering. Try to pair native plants from your region with your design, so that the garden blends in well with your environment but

60

the flowers and plants will survive the natural conditions without issue.

Succulents seem fragile, but they can handle dry conditions well with very little maintenance. So, if you want them, add some succulents to your rock garden.

You can let this rock garden design blend seamlessly into the natural landscape of your home. However, if you want to edge your garden or make an edge treatment around a walking path, a rock of rocks can separate your plants from the surrounding environment.

ROCK GARDEN

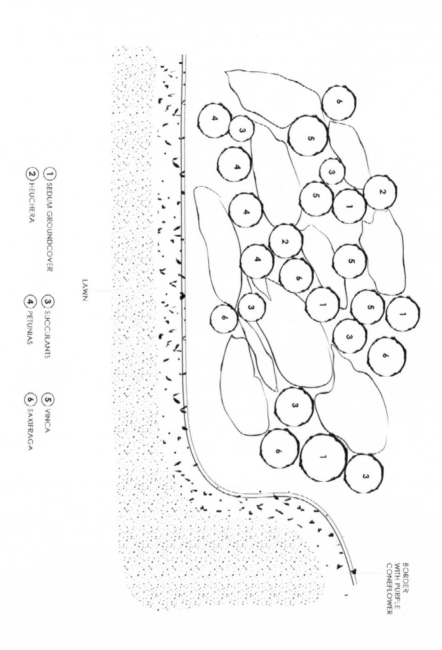

LAWN

BORDER WITH PURPLE CONEFLOWER

1 SEDUM GROUNDCOVER
2 HEUCHERA
3 SUCCULENTS
4 PETUNIAS
5 VINCA
6 SAXIFRAGA

Chapter Twelve

Zen Garden Design

A Zen garden is a style of rock garden from Japan, or a "dry landscape" garden. Here your goal is to create a miniature landscape by carefully composing different arrangements of moss, rocks, water features, pruned trees, and sand or gravel raked in such a way that it looks like ripples in the water. Zen gardens are typically small, surrounded by a while. Zen gardens are supposed to be seen while sitting form a single lookout point like your porch. Here you are meant to meditate on life's purpose and the influence of nature.

That said, Zen garden designs reflect the spiritual aspect of Buddhism and typically include a shallow, enclosed sandbox with sand or rocks of different sizes. Rocks and sand are the main elements in your garden, creating a scene of different "islands" in the sea. The sand itself represents the ocean and your other elements are the islands. With a Zen garden, you can include many bonsai trees that are carefully pruned, large Ginkgo trees that give off a beautiful yellow color when they bloom, and moss. You do not, though, need to put many plant or flower species.

Traditionally, you would plant bright yellow plants for the yang energy and dark green plants for your yin energy.

The most important thing here is to arrange your garden so that it is pleasing to the eye so that you can relax. Consider the size of the space you have. You do not have to allocate all of your backyard to a Zen garden design. You can create a small Zen garden in one part of your yard, or transform your entire space. You are going to need a lot of sand and wherever you put sand, put a wood border or box to keep it contained. Rake your sand once you have it in place. Create curved strokes, ripple patterns. Rake the sand three to four inches deep to get the best look. Remember, too, you can change the style and patterns any time you want.

Add stones and pebbles to the garden. Arrange them well. If you have large rocks, submerge them partially in your sandbox. Don't put too many of them in one place or it will look cluttered. You can place them off-center or stack three in the middle around which you rake the sand. Add Zen features like a stone Buddha, rock boulder, statue, or anything else that you prefer. Incorporate some plants and be sure to build a clear path through the garden. Stone paths are a great way to add to the design.

Not all Zen gardens are dry. You can add ponds, water features, and in so doing add positive energy to the garden. If you incorporate water, such as a small stream or pond, investing in large boulders that rise a few inches above the water and complete your path across the water is best.

Build a Bridge

If you have a stream running through your garden or you have installed a pond as part of your Zen garden design, a walking bridge is important. Small footbridges add atmosphere and character to a Zen garden. Exotic hardwood is the best option for the structures as it is almost impervious to water damage and implement weather. Adding a Bridge to the walking path through your Zen garden will help to create a relaxed mood and of course still be functional. Koi ponds are a great place to add bridges. With a small walkway that spans around your Koi pond, and a bridge that goes across you have the opportunity to look down into the water and watch your fish at play. This is not only a source of relaxation for adults but provides children with hours of entertainment.

Lighting is great for larger spaces especially Zen gardens. Before you set up the lights you need to consider how you want your garden to the lit. You might want Japanese lanterns to provide illumination and create atmosphere. If you plan on engaging in family activities, playing outside, you might need brighter lights compared to the small lights you would install along a footpath for Romantic midnight strolls.

When you are creating your small you might want a romantic atmosphere in the garden in which case individual torches give you just enough light to safely walk around during dusk without ruining the mood. However, if you have a deck, bridge, or a wooden walking trail you can get lighting built into a railing system so you can easily follow the path without ruining the atmosphere.

Finally, consider adding a structure like a pagoda or a pergola with a garden bridge and wooden seating areas for relaxation and reflection.

ZEN GARDEN

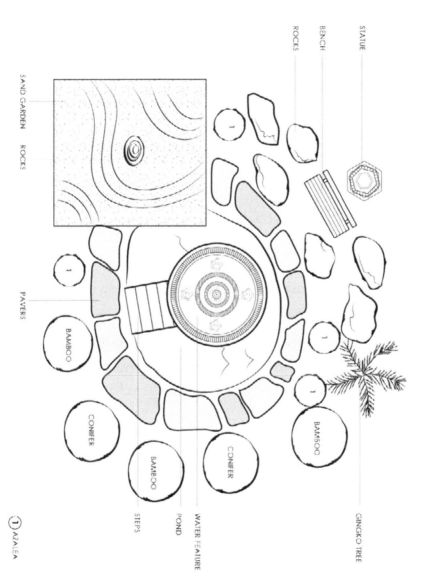

STATUE

BENCH

ROCKS

SAND GARDEN

ROCKS

PAVERS

BAMBOO

CONIFER

BAMBOO

CONIFER

BAMBOO

GINGKO TREE

STEPS

POND

WATER FEATURE

(1) AZALEA

67

Chapter Thirteen

Deck Garden Design

Just because you only have a deck does not mean you cannot have a garden. Even without a sprawling lawn and ample soil to spare, you can capitalize upon container gardening to set up plants and flowers where you want them. Enhance your deck with easy to grow shrubs, even vegetables.

Again, we won't go too much into this because it really requires container gardening and if you want to cultivate food, you need specifics for that. Both are covered in another chapter.

Most people settle for a line of small shrubs, something that makes a border or offers some privacy. However, you can create a great L-shaped garden to help dampen the sounds of a nearby road, incorporate color where there is none, or add fragrance to your relaxation space.

So, set up your pots or containers where you want the plants to be. You won't be able to easily move them once they are filled with soil so either set them up knowing they won't be moved or get some wheel based trays so you can slide them around. If you want to add height, you can install simple flower boxes on a fence.

Once you have the pots in place, start planting what you love best!

That said, you can always make a deck and then create a deck garden design. If you want a deck in your garden you don't have to limit yourself to a flat structure. You can use stairs or trellises to add different layers. There are also many ways to position your deck. If you can, create a seamless transition from inside to outside by a making sure the deck is level with the room leading to it. If your garden is located on a slope this might be somewhat impractical. Instead, you can choose a design one or two different levels for each of the sloped regions. Take note of where the sun hits your garden throughout the day and avoid setting up a deck where it is too hot or too cold. The size is obviously influenced by what you have in mind for the deck. If you want to build in seating around a pond or you want to put a hot tub outside might need a bigger deck. If you want a single space for dining, you might need a deck big enough to hold a barbecue, wash station, and seating. You don't want the deck to constitute the whole of your garden space so make sure you zone appropriately while still giving yourself a room for a lawn or flowers. Make sure the deck is made from durable softwood so that exposure to weather does not damage the integrity. Also, make sure that any stain you use is water repellent so that the color does not change with time. Once the deck is installed consider whether you want plants to soften the edge of the deck. You can plant small shrubs or trees at the corners for around the perimeter or even use containers. If, for example, the outdoor area on your deck is intended specifically for food prep and dining, you might use containers along the perimeter with vegetables and herbs so that you can pick them quickly and cook them.

DECK GARDEN

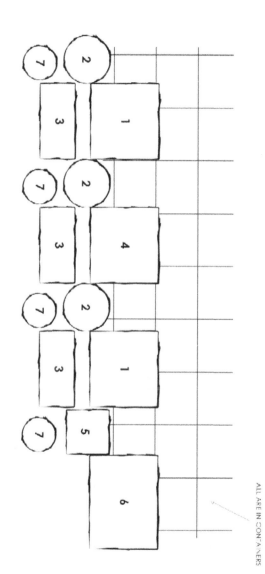

1. BOXWOOD
2. GERANIUMS
3. LAMB'S EAR
4. FOUNTAIN GRASS
5. CANNA
6. LAVENDER
7. SWEET ALYSSUM

ALL ARE IN CONTAINERS

71

Chapter Fourteen

Water Garden Design

A water garden needs to be set up in a place where you will get a minimum of 6 hours of direct sunlight. From there, you need to choose a variety of plants which complement one another in bloom time, color, and height.

Water plants are separated into four distinct groups:

1. Floating plants
2. Bog plants
3. Oxygenating plants
4. And water lilies

Oxygenating plants like cabomba, anacharis, and water milfoil are the most important because they will provide the oxygen needed for your aquatic animals like Koi fish for a Koi pond. They will also compete with algae for carbon dioxide. These plants should be placed at the bottom of your pond. If you have bog plants like papayrus, cattail, or Lobelia cardinalis, rest assured they will add some varying height and color to your water area. They prefer shallow water and will grow along the edge of the pond. Floating plants include water lettuce, floating ferns, and duckweed which will remain on top of the pond and help to shade the things living below. Finally, water lilies are the most commonly identified water plant. They should be planted 6 inches below the surface of the water.

When you plant your water garden, consider mixing perennials around the actual pond and then lining the border with stone coping. You can mix flowers around the pond and add some stepping stones from the water to your garden path or your lawn, or even your home. Then add the oxygenating plants at the bottom, the bog plants along the border sporadically, and the rest on top. You have much room to play around here based on what animals, if any, you want to maintain in your water area. You might want to incorporate a water feature, build a system to pipe water over a small stone wall into the pond, or filter water into multiple ponds and small river systems. You can choose to set up a small water garden inside another garden design, like a Koi pond in your Zen garden design or a water garden with frogs and small fish in your cottage garden design. Again, the choice is up to you and the space you can afford.

Water features

Water features can truly transform your garden design into a place for relaxation and social engagement. Garden water features or things like water lilies can be easily integrated into small ponds. Some more artistic designs can be created with stacked stone. The stacked stone can match the size and shape of your patio or courtyard and provide a natural look for the water feature with the technical aspects in from view. European-style designs tend to add whimsical seating around a classical fountain whereas Asian designs often have a remote-controlled waterfall that is small in size. Be aware of the fact that a water: pond will use a lot of electricity and can add roughly $100 per month to your bill. If you choose to set up a fountain with a timer you can reduce the cost. Ponds are perfect if you want to have fish but the water inside the pond will likely remain green almost all the time as a fight off the algae. If you don't have fish in your pond you can set up a water feature that has chlorinated water the same as a swimming pool and this will give you that clear to you straight down to the bottom.

You can select different sized water garden pumps and use plastic liners to create the wall. Add sand to the pond if you want to adjust a floor. You can also enhance your finished look with ornamental features, rocks, or plants. You might want to include a patio style water feature, a tiered water feature, a statuary feature or a pot style feature. Different materials are available for all of these features including marble, copper, slate, glass, or black onyx.

75

WATER GARDEN

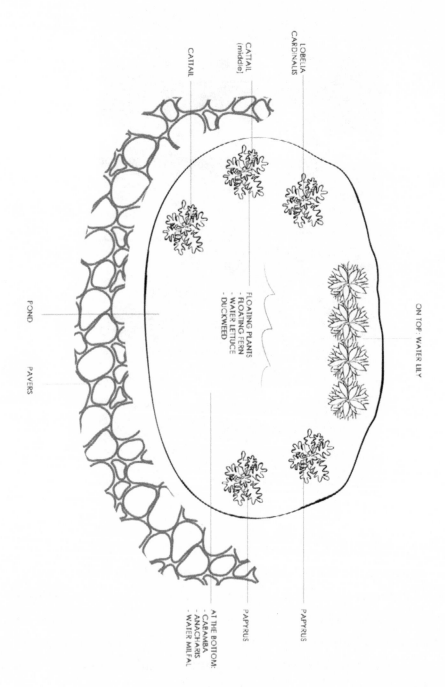

LOBELIA
CARDINALIS

CATTAIL
(middle)

CATTAIL

ON TOP: WATER LILY

FLOATING PLANTS
- FLOATING FERN
- WATER LETTUCE
- DUCKWEED

POND

PAVERS

PAPYRUS

PAPYRUS

AT THE BOTTOM:
- CABAMBA
- ANACHARIS
- WATER MILFAL

Chapter Fifteen

Shade Garden Design

Not every garden is going to get sunlight. Some yards are just not set up for sun exposure, especially in bigger cities. Do not fret! You can still design a shade garden that serves as an escape.

To create your shade garden design, start by reducing grass. Every lawn will struggle and if you live in an area that is shady, don't fight the dying, patch-laden lawn. Keep a small section of turf where the most sunlight falls, then build your landscape around it with shade-loving plants.

Transform your shady spots into a stylish oasis by adding brightly colored flowers and a bench. Having a seating area is very important, as it gives you a place to just sit down with a glass of lemonade on a hot summer day and reflect.

Play around with texture. Make a dramatic statement without flowers by combining plants that offer various textures or colors. For example, you can plant a big leaf umbrella plant next to a golden meadow rue. You can also put an anemone or purple leaf coralbells next to your golden meadow rue.

77

Alternatively, or perhaps concurrently, plant brightly colored flowers to illuminate any dim spots in your yard. Golden Japanese forest grass, for example, can add a shade of gold that really shines in an otherwise dim and dark space. In shady spaces, you should take advantage of groundcover. Groundcover will protect against weeds and make it easier to maintain the space. As a bonus, some groundcover forms a naturally attractive carpet of soft foliage, like the golden creeping Jenny.

Try to incorporate artwork. Quirky objects can give your garden personality. A collection of colorful hanging ornaments, for example, can add a focal point, create charm, and lend to better light dancing across your yard. Find interesting materials too, making the best use of hardscape elements like dark wood chips as a path through your garden, or a mixture of ornamental grasses along the perimeter. Plant flowering shrubs. Hostas, for example, are great for shade gardens. Rhododendrons and azaleas can give your garden a bright springtime color and evergreen foliage stays green all winter long.

Consider adding a water feature if you can fit it/afford it. The sensory appeal is enhanced with the sound of trickling water. All it takes is a simple water fountain and a recirculating pump to make this magic happen. Consider using unique objects like round millstones for old barrels as containers for the plants. These unique architectural elements at a whimsical feel and provide a great accent piece.

When it comes to picking flowers, grow annuals so that you have color inside shady spots. Annuals are great for shade gardens because they will bloom all summer. Try impatiens, iresine, browallia, coleus, torenia, or balsam.

If you have a flower bed for a small path, create a border using an interesting material. Japanese forest grass provides a stunning color and a unique texture. You can also use architectural elements to create your borders like terra-cotta pots or something that reflect your personality. Sprinkle a few plants that you want to be your focal point. The Gold heart bleeding heart for the Japanese maple, for example, provide great texture and create an interesting vignette. Nearly every type of plant you pick will look better if it is in a large group rather than planted individually. So, you don't have to grow a single variety. You might, for example, pick one type of plant and then grow several varieties of that plant. Creating a small space for herbs might mean grouping together red basil, traditional basil, and Thai basil with its unique color patterns. You want to plant shapes that draw the eye, so look for perennials that have straight edge borders to mix around loose mounds of flowing plants.

If you want to take advantage of your shade area, smaller vines can add an extra layer of color and will happily scramble up a tree trunk or create a privacy screen if you have a fence or trellis. For shade gardens, the best vines are Virginia creeper, climbing hydrangea, and Dutchman's pipe.

It is best for a shaded space that you pick only one or two hues and stick with those. So, perhaps green foliage against pink and red tones, for example.

On the note of climbing vines, they also add height, and that is important. Many shade gardens have low perennials growing under tall trees. Try to add some tall planters or put a medium height shrub, even a pillar to offset these distinct heights.

If you have oval shapes for your plants, consider rectangular pavers for a path. Mixing materials and geometric shapes can help draw the eye.

SHADE GARDEN

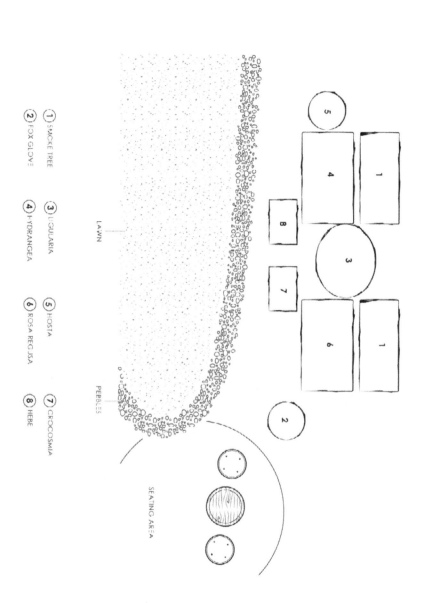

LAWN

PEBBLES

SEATING AREA

1. SMOKE TREE
2. FOX GLOVE
3. LIGULARIA
4. HYDRANGEA
5. HOSTA
6. ROSA REGUSA
7. CROCOSMIA
8. HEBE

83

Chapter Sixteen

Moon Garden Design

Some people prefer to enjoy their gardens at night, especially those who work odd hours, have a tight schedule, or are just night owls. If this is you, a moon garden design is a wonderful way to enjoy bright whites, comfortable seating, and fragrant blooms.

In order to truly appreciate the magic that encompasses a garden at night time, you have to sit down for at least 10 minutes and let all of your worries fade away while your eyes adjust to the darkness. In a moon garden design after about 10 minutes the light colors and white colors will take on a splendid glow. The green stems and the darker leaves fade into the darkness leaving the blooms to look as though they are floating.

Lighter colors or variegated plants are much more pronounced in the evening. A garden design is conceived much the same as a summer garden but that doesn't mean you should neglect plants that you can enjoy during other seasons. If you live in a climate warm enough to enjoy the moon garden during other seasons, plant things with an architectural form that might give you something interesting to look at even in the dead of winter. Harry Lauder's walking stick is one example.

Night bloomers like four-o'clock's, moonflowers, and angels' trumpets will give your space a special quality while emitting a powerful fragrance that draws night pollinators to your yard. No doubt you will hear the swishing of your foliage mixed with the light hum of these creatures.

When you set up a moon garden you need to make a place to sit and enjoy your view. This is really the purpose of having such a garden. Placing a bench along the perimeter will give you a fuller view, but you might prefer some chairs right in the center. Some people like the freedom to look up at the moon and stars above them, while others live in areas prone to rain so a pergola or covered seating area is best. Wrought iron is the most popular furniture material for moon gardens, but don't forget about the cushions. Your seating won't be conducive to relaxation if you forget the cushions.

The moon garden is also something you can incorporate into a larger space. If, again, you have a large garden and you cordon it off into sections, you can allocate one space for the moon garden.

MOON GARDEN

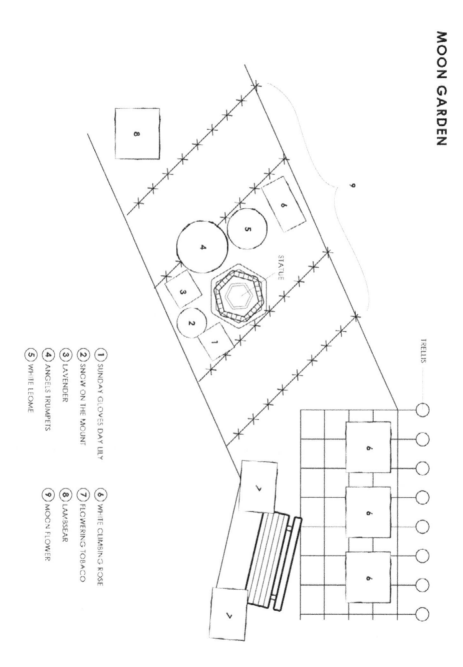

STATUE

TRELLIS

① SUNDAY GLOVES DAY LILY
② SNOW ON THE MOUNT
③ LAVENDER
④ ANGELS TRUMPETS
⑤ WHITE LEOME

⑥ WHITE CLIMBING ROSE
⑦ FLOWERING TOBACO
⑧ LAMBSEAR
⑨ MOON FLOWER

87

Chapter Seventeen

Woodland Garden Design

Do you an unused wooded space in your yard? Does your yard boast large trees? If so, you can put these natural elements to use by creating a woodland garden design. This design offers a natural appearance that is more relaxed.

For this design, start by taking cues from the natural landscape around you. What native plants are there, what is the soil like, the drainage, how to the plants in your area grow?

With a woodland space, you want to add smaller trees and shrubs first, regardless of where in the space you plan to put them. Then, you can plant the understory plantings. If you are keen, add a birdbath, or bench as a feature piece.

In addition to the shrubs and trees you select, you can add ground cover or moss to complete the feel. Feathery plants with broad leaves are best. If you pick natural woodland plants, you won't have to do much in the way of tending to them, save for the occasional pruning here and there.

Your woodland garden does not take up a lot of space. Using clever designs and incorporating shrubs means you can create shade needed for diminutive flowers that bloom in the spring even with limited space. To create shade for an intimate feel, start with deciduous shrubs that suit your location and your soil. For fertile soil, pick a fragrant witch hazel or Hamamelis x intermedia 'Pallida'. If you poor soil, you can still get pink and white flowers with the Viburnum x burkwoodii, or some oranges with the Philadelphus coronarius 'Aureus'. Once you have the shrubs, plant right up against its main stem with non-invasive plants that flower in the spring. The oriental hellebore is great, as is the miniature narcissi or scillas.

Remember too that after spring and summer have set, most of the blooming plants will fade away, so you want to incorporate some plants that offer a year-round presence.

Woodland Garden Plants

If you want spring flowering woodland plants, then consider the Galanthus elwesii. This plant has grey leaves and will bloom from January onward. The Narcissus 'Elka' is a miniature daffodil that has a pale cream trumpet and white petals. It will start to bloom in March. A Scilla siberica has cobalt blue miniature bulbs and bright verdant foliage. The stems are dark and have three miniature bells on them. Scilla mischtschenkoana is a more ice blue color and it will hug the ground. Use this as a great piece of groundcover because it will flower in the snowy weather. For April blooms, consider the Erythronium 'White Beauty' which reaches about one foot high and has a marbled white and chocolate appearance. Conversely, the Crocus 'Yalta' is purple and silver gray. When the buds open up they have a bright orange center. For hyacinths, consider the Muscari aucheri 'Blue Magic' which is non-invasive, with bright blue flowers boasting a white rim. For something pink, try the Cyclamen coum which has a magenta tipped, pink flower that sits atop round leaves. The Iris reticulata 'Harmony' is absolutely beautiful with early springtime blooms of blue crested in white and yellow.

If you want spring woodlanders that are noninvasive, the Anemone nemorosa 'Robinsoniana' offers round petals that are a light blue and they flower later in the spring. Euphorbia polychrome creates acid-yellow flowers that are set to bloom each March-April, offset by the blue bulbs. Pulmonaria 'Blue Ensign' is deep blue, with violent spears. Bees love these flowers when they open in April, so if you are a fan of bees, plant some of these.

As far as the pulmonaria are concerned, the Pulmonaria 'Diane Clare' is the best option for you with violet flowers blooming in March and apple-green leaves with just a hint of silver. The Primula 'Hall Barn Blue' give you yellow-eyed, blue flowers for most of the spring. These are easy to care for as well. A very special consideration is the Bergenia 'Overture' which offers red leaves and bright pink flowers. With blue flowers and silver-marbled foliage, you can plant the aptly named Brunnera 'Jack Frost'. If you need a short woodlander, consider the tiny blue flowers set against a white edge that bloom from Omphaloides cappadocica 'Starry Eyes'.

Of course, if you prefer to have woodland plants all year round, not just in spring, then the Sarcococca confuse is your winner. This plant has ivory white flowers and green foliage. Creamy flowers that stem from the triangular buds are the result of Skimmia x confusa 'Kew Green'. You can plant Euphorbia amygdaloides 'Purpurea' for lime green and beetroot foliage. Ice pink flowers combined with verdant foliage is offered by Daphne 'Eternal Fragrance'. For a taller, columnar plant, try planting the Daphne 'Jacqueline Postill'. You will get very fragrant pink flower clusters in January and evergreen foliage the rest of the year. Bright green leaves will be afforded by the Asplenium scolopendrium 'Kaye's Lacerated' if you can plant it somewhere in the shade. A holly fern is another option, like the Polystichum tsussimense. The Daphne 'Rebecca' can be planted for green foliage lined in yellow. It will produce flowers in early spring. Buxus sempervirens is a useful evergreen along the edges of your woodland garden. The foliage has an olive green tinge and is always glossy.

WOODLAND GARDEN

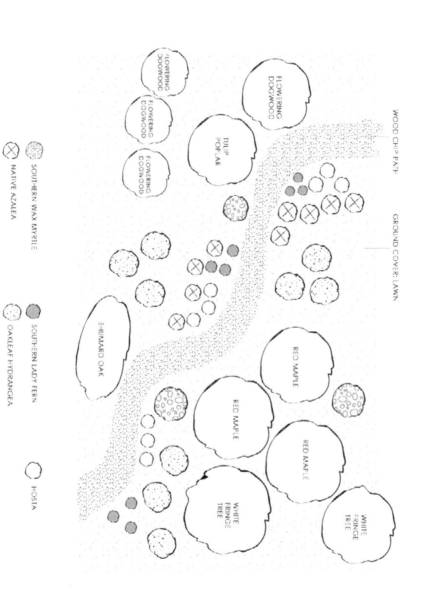

WOOD CHIP PATH

GROUND COVER: LAWN

FLOWERING DOGWOOD

FLOWERING DOGWOOD

FLOWERING DOGWOOD

FLOWERING DOGWOOD

TULIP POPLAR

SHUMARD OAK

RED MAPLE

RED MAPLE

RED MAPLE

WHITE FRINGE TREE

WHITE FRINGE TREE

SOUTHERN WAX MYRTLE

NATIVE AZALEA

SOUTHERN LADY FERN

OAKLEAF HYDRANGEA

HOSTA

93

Chapter Eighteen

Wildlife Garden Design

For those love and adore the animals that nature has to offer, a wildlife garden design might be a great way to encourage their visits. Birds, bees, and butterflies will flock to your garden if you plant things that they love. If your space is limited, you can make a tiny garden corner in your yard and soon it will act as a wildlife refuge. Before you plant though, figure out what birds or butterflies reside in your native area and find the plants that work best for them. If, for example, hummingbirds are normal, plant brightly colored, tube-shaped flowers like red salvia, trumpet vine, or bee balm. If you want to bring butterflies to your back porch, plant sedum, zinnia, buddleia, or parsley. To add a cacophony of songbirds, plant seed and berry producing flowers, trees, or shrubs.

In a corner space, for example, your lawn can serve as the border. For the 90 degree angle, you can plant arborvitae hedge and round off the border with your lawn using pots of geraniums. Place stepping stones from the center to the corner where you can hang a nice birdhouse. Dot the remaining space with things like pink hydrangeas, pink astilbe, Astrantia, Iris, and Autumn Joy Sedum.

The nice thing about a wildlife garden design is that it does not have to be a standalone design. You can choose to divide a large garden space into a central lawn and then have one corner as a wildlife retreat, one corner as a water garden, one corner for moonlight strolls, and another corner for a seating area. As you read more and more you will find ideas that spark your interest, things you want to add to one design over another. Do not let a single design stifle your creativity. If you want to mix and match, have at it.

WILDLIFE GARDEN

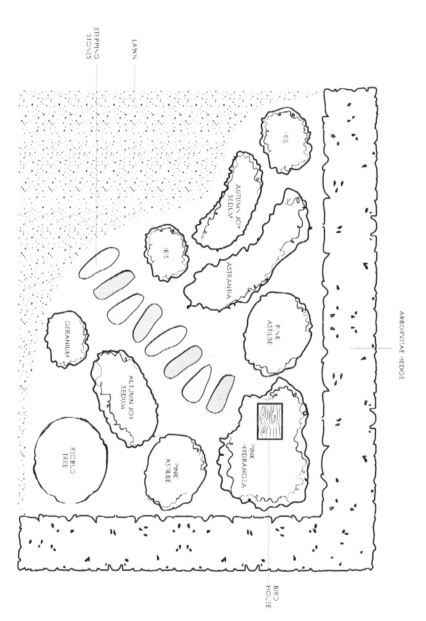

STEPPING
STONES

LAWN

IRIS

AUTUMN JOY
SEDUM

IRIS

ASTRANTIA

GERANIUM

PINK
ASTILBE

AUTUMN JOY
SEDUM

ARBORVITAE HEDGE

REDBUD
TREE

PINK
ASTILBE

PINK
HYDRANGEA

BIRD
HOUSE

Chapter Nineteen

Wildflower Garden Design

Wildflower garden designs are a natural combination, especially when set against a backdrop of native grasses. You can enjoy a traditional design that takes advantage of the wildflowers and native grasses in your area.

To start, plant these two things together. The native grasses and wildflowers create a natural meadow. The grasses have dense root systems so they dominate the upper soil and prevent weeds from growing. Wild grasses do almost all of the weeding for you.

Pick plants that fit with the scale of your yard. If you have a smaller garden space, use shorter flowers and grasses. If you plant Prairie Dropseed, Side Oats Grama, or Little Bluestem they will grow in clusters and won't really leave room for lots of flowers, so be sure to separate the wildflowers here from your clusters. Try to incorporate deep-rooted wildflowers to offset this sort of plant bullying. Deep roots will grow more than 10 feet down below the grassroots so that both can share the water and nutrients in the soil.

In order to create impact in your garden, plant the flowers in masses of color. Arrange your plants so that they complement one another both in terms of texture and in color. For example, plant Prairie Dock behind the flowering spikes of Blazingstars. Many of the grasses and wildflowers provide great green shades that serve as a backdrop against which bright blooms rest.

Think about your yard all year. You don't want blooms for just a few months, so plant things that will grow in succession, some flower right after the others. The grasses, of course, will still give you that nice green color during the winter. Plant tall plants along wooden fences, walls, or in the back of your garden space and then shorter plants in front. Then pick one large plant as your focal point and set up the other plants around it.

If you have a particularly dry soil you can plant smooth aster, sky blue aster, lancelead coreopsis, or butterflyweed. If you have a

99

medium or moist soil you can plant great blue lobelia, smooth penstemon, spiderwort, rattlesnake master, or prairie blazingstar. Spring blooming wildflowers include Lupine, Wild Iris, Shootingstar, Golden Alexanders, Spiderwort, and Jack in the pulpit. Deep-rooted flowers to add to your grasses include things like Rattlesnake master, cupplant, yellow coneflower, purple prairie clover, wild quinine, leadplant, butterflyweed, wild senna, and pale purple coneflower. For your focal point plant, consider culver's root, blue false indigo, joe pye wood, or Queen of the Prairie plants.

The nice thing about adding spring-blooming wildflowers is that you will attract wildlife like songbirds and butterflies. These will only enhance your garden space. The blooms give nectar for the butterflies and the songbirds love the seeds from grasses, silphiums, or sunflowers. By integrating natural flowers and grasses you won't need special irrigation, fertilizers, or pesticides because the plants are already designed to thrive in your environment.

WILDFLOWER

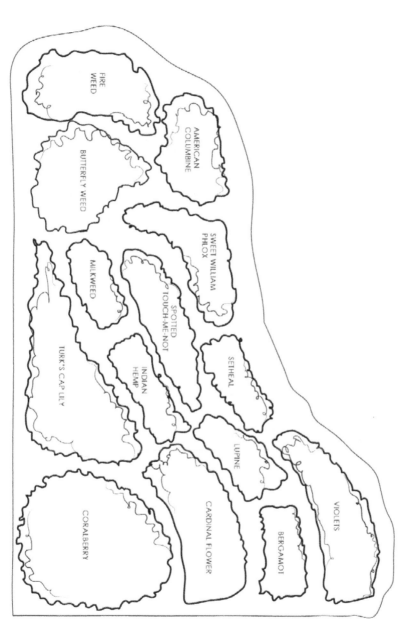

FIRE WEED

AMERICAN COLUMBINE

BUTTERFLY WEED

SWEET WILLIAM PHLOX

MILKWEED

SPOTTED TOUCH-ME-NOT

TURK'S CAP LILY

INDIAN HEMP

SETHEAL

LUPINE

CORALBERRY

CARDINAL FLOWER

BERGAMOT

VIOLETS

Chapter Twenty

Vertical and Container Garden Design - Growing Food at Home

Vertical Garden Design

Vertical gardens are a popular new gardening trend that happens to be one of the oldest gardening designs out there. Anyone who is ever grown up fine on a trellis or fence understands how old vertical gardening really is. Vertical gardening is a great solution for smaller outdoor spaces and indoor spaces. People who live in apartments or have very strict landlords for their home and are not afforded the opportunity to create a large, sprawling outdoor garden space can still enjoy a vertical garden.

Vertical gardening is a wonderful way to take advantage of small spaces in your home, garden, balcony, interior, or any other place you can manage. You can maximize the yield you get from fruits and vegetables in your home when you use vertical gardening indoors or out. The nice thing about such a set-up is that you can create a living wall inside your home or set up fruits and vegetables outside too, creating a tall garden around whatever small space you have available.

With vertical gardening, you are simply growing a garden upward instead of across a flat parcel of land. This might mean using containers (more on this later) and affixing them a few feet on top of one another up an existing wall, or installing a fence against which containers are placed upright, or even growing plants which climb naturally and simply using netting or an existing fence or wall to allow the stems to grow upward. You can use traditional watering techniques, install water drip lines, or set up alternative watering systems all based on the design of the garden you select. Try not to think of vertical gardening as a single thing, but rather, as a way to take advantage of all space in a small gardening area and produce the most fruits or vegetables.

You can grow rows and rows of your favorite roots vegetables at the base of any vertical garden, with other leafy vegetables in containers placed on top. You can grow one or two climbing items like tomatoes or beans and add a trellis so that they can climb upward against the exterior wall of your home. The possibilities are endless.

The key is to ensure there is adequate support for whatever you are growing. If you have eight planter boxes of herbs affixed to a wall on top of one another, leave enough space in between for the herbs to thrive. If you are planting cucumbers and want to train them up the trellis against your backyard wall, be sure to have a strong enough trellis for the fully mature plants. Many of the climbing plants like tomatoes and cucumbers will keep growing until you stop them. You can, of course, snip them at a certain height to keep your neighbors from getting annoyed.

Many of the elements of a vertical garden will draw attention to a specific area that you wish to enhance or disguise an unattractive view you want to cover up. With vertical gardening, you want structures or call him like trees to create vertical rooms or hidden spaces. Trellises can be attached to the ground or attached to a large container so that you can grow vegetables, flowers, and binds using much less space than a traditional garden requires. This type of vertical container gardening is perfect for rooftop gardens, apartments with very small balconies, deck gardens, and much more. Vertical gardening is a great way for disabled gardeners, small space dwellers, and even gardeners who have traditional spaces to use upright structures.

If your only space is available indoors, you can grow small stature houseplants as part of your vertical garden and create a living wall. This living wall will not only provide a physical tapestry of color and a variety of textures but it will help to naturally filter any air pollutants out of your indoor air. If you live in a cold winter climate, having houseplants like this will add humidity during the months when your furnace will dry out the air. They do need more frequent watering than other forms of gardening but vertical garden designs contribute to good air circulation indoors and outdoors.

Green walls are one form of vertical gardens which cover your wall with climbing plants. In your existing space, if you have a wall that you wish to conceal or brighten, a green wall is the perfect solution. This allows plants to grow up or, creating a sort of screen.

The trick to this particular type of garden design is really using whatever materials best fit your preferences. For example, if you have an outdoor space or even an indoor space that is very modern, you might want to invest in pre-designed vertical garden kits that have all the components already built for you in a certain color and material. If you are more flexible and you want something that has character to it, perhaps something that fits a cottage style garden, you can bolt together a metal or wood frame and hang it on your wall or let it stand alone in your garden. Rigid plastic attached to a frame makes your vertical garden waterproof, in case you are growing things up against an existing structure. More creative ideas take regular pots for containers and simply affix them to several points horizontally and vertically up the wall.

If you consider a section of trellis, the wood beams are already affixed to one another evenly spaced horizontally and vertically. At each point where the vertical and horizontal lines cross, you can attach a hook and hang a container. Then you fill each of the containers with potting soil and grow your small plants, herbs, or flowers. Vertical gardening like this allows you to create living paintings. If your garden is green and green alone, you can plant all green things in your vertical garden design. If the space uses bright red flowers and bright purple flowers, you can plant complementary colors along the border of the vertical wall, or in a diagonal design. Whatever you decide, vertical garden designs need irrigation systems and you will still have to tend it to whatever you plant to fertilize it, prune the plants, we eat at the plants, sometimes even replace them. Also, bear in mind that vertical gardens are very heavy especially after you have planted everything so always check with a structural expert to make sure that whatever wall you're going to place your garden upon can handle this load.

If you are using a vertical gardening design outdoors, anchor the structure in place before you plant anything so that you avoid disturbing any of the stands or roots of your plants. Make sure you pair heavier or more demanding plants with a sturdier structure. Also, take into consideration the taller plants will cast a shadow on your vertical garden which could impact the growing patterns of plants in the nearby vicinity.

Plants will grow differently in a vertical garden. Things like climbing roses need to physically attach to structures whereas other plants like morning glories will loop around themselves and any trellis opening. The plants you choose might require more water and fertilization than normal because they will be exposed to more wind and more light in a vertical gardening design.

There are a variety of plants you can use for vertical gardening designs contingent upon the light conditions you have where you live. For traditional gardening consider annual flowering vines which climb but don't get too heavy like the Cardinal climber, moonflower, black-eyed Susan Vine, Cyprus vine, or hyacinth bean. These all grow best in full sunlight.

Perennial vines that you might consider include ivy, American bittersweet, or clematis hybrids which all grow best in the full sun. However, clematis prefer the flowers to be in the sun but their roots to be in the shade.

If you have a shaded area for your vertical garden if you have a shade of vertical garden you can grow the hearty kiwi, climbing hydrangea, Siberian gooseberries, edible flowers, or vegetables like tomatoes, pole beans, or vining nasturtiums.

If you want to build the structure for your vertical garden yourself, you can use an existing structure like a shed or garage and simply place a trellis in front of one of the walls. You can also use obelisks, arbors, and fences.

Hanging baskets are an important element to vertical gardening because they break up the horizontal plane. You will want to attach a drip irrigation system to make it much easier to water or, conversely, set up a rope and pulley system so that you can access each of the hanging baskets much easier when it is time to water them. Always make sure you leave enough space between multiple trellises for air circulation.

Indoor Vertical Gardens

What to Grow

Inside of your home, you can grow items which require minimal sunlight. Tomatoes, all variety of peppers, herbs, and beans are a great fit for the indoors. Outside of your home, you can grow whatever is best suited for the sunlight and climate in which you live.

There are some recommendations for fruits and vegetables. Vertical gardens are quite versatile and that means that you can technically grow whatever you want depending on how you create your garden. Dwarf varieties of fruit trees, for example, can be trained against a wall or into espaliers. Vine vegetables can be grown vertically so long as you have sufficient support. Root vegetables can be grown too with enough depth.

Tall plants like beans need a method of support, something they can climb up which can protect them against damage. A wire mesh laid against a wall is ideal for climbing plants as it offers the plant plenty of options for training against the wall through the mesh while offering protection to the plants as well.

If you are planting in containers you should keep in mind the weight of your crops, especially if you are going to fix them to a wall or a fence. We will cover more on this in the next section.

Tumbling plant varieties like tomatoes are great for vertical gardens. Strawberries or peas will do well in hanging baskets and can be affixed to the walls or fences around your home or inside.

Herbs are perhaps the best item to use in a vertical garden, and the best-suited item for a beginner because they can be affixed in your kitchen within arms' reach while cooking. You can plant them in small pots and collect the pots in the same area to make for easy access, more on this later.

Tips for planning

Planting anything, whether it is in a vertical garden or in a small container requires some thinking and planning ahead of time. You want to ensure you have the right space and structure for the exact things you are planting because one size does not necessarily fit all plants. It is for this reason that the next sections on container gardening will pay more attention to selecting the right containers (for vertical gardening or non-vertical gardening) and how to properly set up your garden structure.

Sunlight

Selecting the location where your vertical garden will live if it is indoors is not as challenging as it is compared to large outdoor gardens. With a small space, you can take advantage of planter boxes, pots, and containers and move your fruits and vegetables anywhere you want and still maintain their height. You can, of course, create a garden whose contents grow upward in a small yard space too so that your front or back yard both house the foods you need.

Plants need sunlight. The fruits and vegetables you decide to plant whether they are strawberries, kale, onions, herbs, beets, tomatoes, or anything else, require sunlight. The more sunlight they receive, the better. Some plants need up to six hours of sun per day. This is referred to as full sun. Vegetables love to spend the majority of their day in the sun. Of course, if you live in a dry area, you want to ensure your plants get some shady breaks in between their day of sunshine to avoid drying out and burning.

While your home balcony might enjoy a lot of sunlight now, remember to consider the surrounding landscape.

Take these things into consideration and be prepared to move some of your vertical containers if necessary when the seasons change. If you pick an ideal location on your patio which will be blocked by the summer trees, then consider moving it to another location each summer or just moving it elsewhere permanently.

Each location will receive a different amount of sun during different times of the day. Once you know the location where you will start your small space garden, you can figure out how many hours of sun it receives.

Full Sun (FS) is a category of sunlight which means six hours of direct sun each day. Partial Sun is another category which refers to less than five hours of direct sunlight each day. Partial Shade (PS) is where your area receives between two and four hours of sunlight.

Shade constitutes an area where you receive less than 1 hour of direct sunlight each day.

Below is a list of fruits and vegetables which require full sun versus partial sun:

Full Sun (FS)

- Beans
- Carrots
- Corn
- Potatoes
- Sweet potatoes
- Beets
- Grains
- Peas
- Radishes
- Hibiscus
- Spinach
- Cucumbers
- Eggplant
- Squash
- Bell pepper
- Tomatoes

Full Sun/or Partial Sun (PS)

- Kale
- Broccoli
- Cabbage
- Okra
- Cauliflower
- Brussels Sprouts
- Celery

Partial Sun (PS)

- Pepper
- Turnips
- Collards
- Lettuce
- Mustard greens

Watering

Watering your fruits and vegetables are what keep them happy and healthy. All plants require water but vegetables require just a bit more. Some plants need water twice per day, while others do not. There are a few factors which influence this.

The size of your garden will influence the regularity with which plants must be watered. The temperature outside will influence it as well. If it is particularly hot one day versus raining another, you might need to increase or decrease the amount you water. The sunlight can dictate how dry your plants get. If it is quite sunny, your fruits and vegetables may need more water than normal. The humidity can impact dryness in the soil and how much water the roots of your plants absorb. The plant itself may have very different requirements. Peppers, for example, require less water than tomatoes or beans.

In order to tell if your foods need water, stick your finger into the soil up to the first knuckle. If the soil is wet, you can skip that round of watering. If the soil is dry all the way up to your first knuckle, it needs water.

If you give your fruits and vegetables too much water, they will drown. If you give them too little they will dry out. You need to make sure no excess moisture remains in your container before you give your foods new water. If the soil becomes soggy, it will stunt the growth of your plants and lead to decay.

If possible, you want to water your fruits and vegetables in the morning so that the water does not evaporate under the sunlight immediately regardless of where they are located. You also want the plants to be dry before the cold evening air sets in. By watering in the morning, you can prevent harmful fungus from accumulating. When you are adding water, add it slowly until the water begins to drip out of the bottom holes. If you can, use a nozzle or watering can with the multiple holes in lieu of a single stream so that it softly covers the whole of the plant rather than fiercely piercing the soil and harming the roots.

If you are overly cautious and fearful of water loss because of evaporation, you can mulch your fruits and vegetables using dry grass, organic compost, or small pebbles.

Soil Quality

Good soil is essential for good fruits and vegetables if you are planting a vertical garden. When you are growing vegetables in containers it is even more important that you have soil which drains well and is aerated. You need soil which can simultaneously retain large amounts of moisture for extended periods of time.

If you are planting the fruits and vegetables in a garden with a trellis, you can use the soil already there and add some compost or fertilizer, but if you are growing your garden in pots, you need to make a new mixture. If you choose to take some soil from your existing yard, make sure you mix one part builder sand or one part perlite. Never, ever use beach sand in your garden.

Lightweight and porous mixtures will improve water content quality and drainage systems for your containers. In fact, the best soil mixture is one which remains loose, allows water to drain, adds nutrition to the roots, and retains moisture. If you are using commercial soil mixtures, be sure to check if it has chemical additives. If so, stay away. Rely on organic fertilizers like compost, fish weed emulsions, earthworm castings, or garden fertilizers.

If you wish to make your own mixture you can read more about this is the container sections.

We will touch more upon selecting seeds in the container sections.

Seeds

When you start out cultivating your small space garden, regardless of whether you are using planter boxes or small containers, you can either buy seeds from a local gardening store or produce seeds yourself from your first crops.

If you choose to purchase seeds from a local store you want to first decide on the plants that you wish to cultivate. Think about the fruits and vegetables that you often eat. Consider the time it takes for the fruits or vegetables to manifest. Raspberries, for example, which can be trained to wind up a vertical garden, take two years of gardening before they will bear fruit. Once you have your preliminary list of things, it is important to check on when they should be planted. If you are getting seeds for carrots, you cannot plant them in the early spring. But if you have strawberries on your list of things you want to grow, you can start those in early spring. You will need to create a sort of schedule for your planting.

Find out first what items you want to grow which are perennial, which mean they live for more than two years. Strawberries, for example, are perennials, so you might decide to grow them from seed and leave them in their containers year after year. Other perennials include ginger, oregano, sage, basil, rosemary, tomatoes, sweet potatoes, potatoes, kale, rhubarb, leek, watercress, and peppermint. So items like these can be left in their containers all year round.

But items which are seasonal you might want to rotate out throughout the year. You might, for example, start planting some peppers and when those are all consumed, replacing those peppers with carrots. Knowing the planting dates of the fruits and vegetables you enjoy consuming, and deciding which plants you want to go in containers as perennial and which will be rotated will help you buy seeds accordingly. Of course, you might just want to save yourself the time and buy all of the seeds you want at once.

That being said, when you are buying seeds, ask if the seeds mature early or late, and whether they result in large or small plants. You might want to know ahead of time if the seeds you are buying for your small bathroom container will manifest into something large and unruly.

Look for seeds with detailed information printed on the package. Reliable seeds will tell you when you can start germinating the foods indoors, when to plant them in containers, when to plant them in the ground, when you should expect blooms, what size they will become, what water and sun exposure they need, how far apart to plant each seed, etc.... If the container lacks this information, try another variety. Never purchase seeds without adequate information.

If you are buying from a store and some of the seed packets seem faded or have been damaged, avoid these. They might have been placed in an area with too much sun exposure which could damage them. Avoid any expired seeds. If possible, search for non-GMO and organic local seeds. These are the healthiest for any small space garden.

If you want to source your own seeds, read about sourcing seeds from previous crops in the sections on container gardening.

Container Garden Design

With containers, you get the option of designing an entire garden around them or integrating them into one of the other garden designs listed. For example, if you decide a design on your deck you might be limited to containers along in which case you will need to not only review the notes for the deck designs but review the notes here so that you can set up what it is you need where you need them. The same is true for some of the other designs like the rooftop designs. The rooftop designs typically require containers because you cannot very well grow something out of the ground if you are located on the roof.

When you start investigating the containers out there, you will be overwhelmed no doubt by the myriad containers available. Almost all shapes, sizes, colors, designs, detailing, and more can be found if you are willing to look. Even glancing around your home will show you a treasure trove of pots and buckets that you can convert into a container garden. Wastebaskets, bowls, terracotta pots are all viable options for the creative mind.

When you go about deciding upon containers, you need to consider a few key details:

Types of Containers:

If you cannot afford to shop for brand new containers, you can always look around your home for things you can easily convert.

When you are choosing your containers, consider any of the following:

- Clay containers you make yourself or purchase, made from drain tiles, terracotta, or ceramic
- Moulded plastic made of non-toxic materials
- Metal
- Plastic bags
- Pots—both glazed and unglazed
- Stones
- Aquariums
- Washtubs
- Wastebaskets
- Storage bins
- Wine crates
- Shoe holders which rest along the backs of doors and have multiple pockets
- Crates
- Bowls

- Cans
- Baskets
- Urns
- Tubs
- Pans and...
- Old boots—to boot!

You can literally select almost any container that you might otherwise throw away. Do you get coffee in a large can? Save that can and convert it into a garden. Do you have a half-gallon paper milk carton, a gallon milk jug, or large soda bottles? Use them to sow seeds. Do you have an old baby sandbox? Use that for your balcony garden.

You can be a bit more creative about it by growing items in vintage china cups you get from a thrift store or from beautiful china bowls you find. A thrift store is bound to have a large bowl of some sort which has lost the rest of the set but still stands alone as a beautiful and large potential centerpiece. Use this as a container for one or more of your herbs and keep it as a dining room centerpiece!

Old fashioned square bathtubs can be transformed as a kitty-corner decoration and garden, home to all of your vegetables. Old canning jars or enameled bowled can add a dash of green and a delicious fruit or vegetable surprise to a bedroom or living room.

There are so many plants which you can cultivate as a single stalk in one pot, and place them throughout the house. Many people have a small window in the bathroom where plenty of sunlight hits, but they have no idea what to place there. A small tomato plant or a strawberry plant might be just the thing! And it can be planted in any container which matches your décor!

Size:

When selecting a container it is important to pick one which is adequate in size for the fruit or vegetables you want to plant. There are many delicious food items which can be maintained year-round in a small bowl, like herbs. They will grow based on the size they are allocated too. So that small rosemary bush you have growing in the living room can be transplanted at a later date to a bigger pot where it will flourish as a rosemary bush.

Take some time to plan the foods you want to plant and determine the depth and width of the container they need. Almost all seeds today come with instructions for the size they require and whether they are suitably maintained in containers rather than a garden. You can read the back to figure out what best suits the time of year, the size of your containers, and the sun exposure. You might have to put some basil in the backroom where not as much sunlight hits but then place the small cherry tomatoes in the front room where there is more sunlight. It is really up to the layout of your home, where you are placing the containers, and what the size is.

If you are planting seeds first, before moving them to a large pot or container, you can select something small in size. Remember though, that the larger pots container more room for root growth which means more soil and better moisture retention. You really need to select the size of the container based on the needs of the plant.

On that note, take into consideration the watering needs of the foods you want to grow. Some plants need to dry out before they are watered again and this means they are best suited for shallow containers. Other foods need constant moisture which means you should plant them in larger pots which offer more water retention.

Larger pots, which can hold more soil, retain water within the roots and therefore require less watering. If you are not the type of person who remembers to water each day, or you take frequent trips or vacations, larger pots are probably a better idea for your garden.

Avoid using a pot which is too big or too small for your plants. Think of your plants like Goldilocks; they need a container which is just right. Do not trim roots to make a plant fit. Plants do not need extra space to grow. The soil from larger pots will retain water for longer periods of time which means that if you over-water it will result in soggy and rotting roots.

And of course, change up the size of the containers so that your finished garden has some creativity and life to it. If you use the same sized pots for all of your foods it will surely look uniform, but you want the pots to really complement the décor of your home.

Stability:

You need to take into consideration the stability of the pots as well. If you are placing pots on your rooftop or balcony, you might need to anchor the pot into place or strap it down to the pavement to protect it from falling over or breaking.

The shape of the container is what lends to its stability, as a matter of physics. That said, you want to ensure your containers do not allow the plants to tip over. A square container which has a strong base is the most stable container you could find. Inverted traditional pots might seem like a good idea but they tend to fall over easily. Pots with straight sides will be much more stable.

Smaller pots are heavier at the rim which means they will more easily fall over, so avoid placing them precariously on balconies with strong winds or where the wagging tails of a pet might knock them over.

Pots with strong bases can resist the heavy weight of plants quite easily. As a rule, the base of the pot should be more than the height. This brings more stability to the plant.

Materials:

There are many materials available for your pots, which can impact the appearance and the maintenance of the plants.

Containers which are made from porous materials like clay or terracotta will soak up water. This means that your plants will dry out fast and they will likely need double the watering. If you want to use porous containers, it is recommended to use plastic lining so that you can better retain water in the soil. In winter, if water gets into the porous pots it could freeze, causing the pot to crack. During the winter months, keep the pots covered if they are outdoors so as to keep them dry. If you are not using the pots during the winter months, try and turn them upside down to prevent them filling with water or snow. If you do place your porous containers on the ground, cover the rim of the pot. If you leave the rim exposed, water will begin to evaporate which will dry out the plant.

One key advantage to using container gardening for a small space is the mobility afforded to you; you can place a potted container just about anywhere. Of course, if you are using a heavier pot you may not be able to just pick it up and move it somewhere else. This is where casters come into play. If you want to grow a multitude of peppers in a large pot, put casters under the pot beforehand so that you can wheel it around your yard or home as you see fit. This will make it easier to take advantage of the sun exposure, especially during bad weather. If it gets too hot in one area of your home, you can slide the pot somewhere else. If it requires more sunlight, move it toward the sun as the sun moves across the sky.

If you are using more lightweight containers, you can sit them on window sills, set them on wooden dining tables, or even hang them from your ceiling. Cultivating hanging herbs from your kitchen ceiling can make it significantly easier to prepare a tasty dinner.

If you want to make a hanging container garden it is best to make sure that there are no costly possessions located beneath the plants, just in case. Water can easily drip from pots and leave a water-stained mess on your possessions. For hanging gardens in small spaces, you also want to ensure each plant is tightly tethered before you hang them and walk away.

Color matters with containers. Darker colors will absorb more heat compared to light colors. If you are using dark colors, you want to try and place that pot in the shade. If you keep this pot in the sun for a long period of time it will absorb a great deal of the heat which will then be transferred to the roots of your plants. This can impede plant growth. If you select a metal container it will alter the temperature of the soil based on the temperature of the metal. This fluctuation might seem minimal to the touch but it can cause serious ramifications for the plant's health. You can control this fluctuation to a degree by insulating the pot with waterproof materials or foam.

Any containers which are treated with chemicals should be avoided at all costs. This defeats the entire purpose of growing your own foods in your small space. If you are using a wood container, make sure it has not been treated with anything either. Because wood decays, some containers are treated with chemicals. But you can instead invest in cedar or redwood containers to offset this otherwise rapid decay and avoid a chemically treated container. It is always good to avoid plastic if you are worried about your carbon footprint.

When selecting your containers you want to find strong containers, well-built enough to hold the plant you want and its roots.

Note

If you are using any form of plastic containers, or you are re-using plastic containers from previous years, you will be better off cleaning them and sterilizing them before you put in any new plants, especially if you are germinating seedlings. It is imperative that any new seeds you want to germinate be placed in sterilized containers. You can do this by:

First washing the containers out to remove any excess debris or dirt.

Then fill a bucket or container large enough to hold the containers for your plants with one part bleach to ten parts water. Leave the containers in there for 30 minutes.

After 30 minutes, wash each container out with soap and water. Allow them to air dry.

Drainage:

Not all pots or containers you purchase will come equipped with the right drainage. This is especially true of containers which you make from items in your home. While you might opt to use a regular bowl or old canning jar, you have to make sure you implement drainage by way of either drilling holes into the bottom of the container or placing things like rocks or moss at the bottom as a barrier between the bottom of the container and the plant roots. This will allow you to check the moisture and determine whether the roots need more water.

Year-Round Gardening

One of the nicest benefits of this form of gardening is that you can garden and yield delicious results all year round. You don't have to buy new containers when it is time to plant something new. Instead, you can just recycle your old pots when the season changes. With containers, you can choose to rearrange your plants throughout the year in different pots or in different arrangements. One year you might hang your herbs from the kitchen ceiling while the next year you might decide to re-pot all of your annual herbs in a single large pot which sits in the kitchen corner.

During the summer you want to use larger containers, if possible, for your smaller plants too so that they retain more moisture. This is especially true if you live somewhere with hotter summer months.

In the autumn you can add a splash of color to your small garden space with beets and chard or even kale. These are all great autumn plants which can rest indoors or outdoors in a small garden space or in a pot.

Making Your Containers

- If you are feeling particularly crafty, you can make your own containers to create the perfect space, design, and size. Of course, if you are going to do this, you need to make sure the creations are adequate in terms of moisture, heat, and space.

- If you are going to make your own containers it is best to do so out of concrete. You want to find a pantry mould and then prepare the concrete mix. You will want a small container and a large container in order to make the small space garden planter. The walls of your planter are dependent upon the space between the large container and the small container.

- With general cooking oil and a paintbrush cover the inside of the large container and all its crevices. Oil the outer walls of the small container.

- Fill the large container with the concrete mixture. Make sure you shake the container of concrete mixture to avoid air bubbles.

- Slowly push the small container into the concrete large container in such a way that you are left with one inch of concrete mixture at the bottom. Do not push the small container into the large container entirely or it will alleviate this small gap you need as the base of your small space planter box.

- Place a weight on the inside of the small container and let the concrete set. This will take roughly 48 hours before the small mould can be removed.

- Once it is dry, take away the mould and use a stone to smooth out the rougher edges. You can drill holes into the bottom of the concrete for drainage or place a piece of cork or foam on the inside of the mould when you are laying the mixture to create the holes you need.

Of course, concrete is not the only thing available. You can convert old books by cutting holes in the center of them. You can create fully organic newspaper containers too. If you want to hang your garden outside or inside, convert old chandeliers such that each point holds a hanging container or holds a painted tin. Avoid using the classic old tires for fruits and vegetables though.

Sunlight

Selecting the location where your containers will live is not as challenging as it is compared to large outdoor gardens. With a small space, you can take advantage of planter boxes, pots, and containers and move your fruits and vegetables anywhere you want. You can create a garden inside or outside. You can design the garden to meet your needs without having to worry about the space or soil quality.

Plants need sunlight. The fruits and vegetables you decide to plant whether they are strawberries, kale, onions, herbs, beets, tomatoes, or anything else, require sunlight. The more sunlight they receive, the better. Some plants need up to six hours of sun per day. This is referred to as full sun. Vegetables love to spend the majority of their day in the sun. Of course, if you live in a dry area, you want to ensure your plants get some shady breaks in between their day of sunshine to avoid drying out and burning.

While your home balcony might enjoy a lot of sunlight now, remember to consider the surrounding landscape. Do you have trees along your home property which bloom with large leaves and flowers and block the sunlight accessible on your balcony in summer? Do you live in an area where your small garden space is surrounded by flowers or bushes which might block small containers from accessing the sunlight year round?

Take these things into consideration and be prepared to move some of your pots or containers if necessary when the seasons change. If you pick an ideal location on your patio which will be blocked by the summer trees, then consider moving it to another location each summer or just moving it elsewhere permanently.

Watering

Watering your fruits and vegetables are what keep them happy and healthy. All plants require water but vegetables require just a bit more. One thing to keep in mind with pots is that each pot might have different levels of drainage. That large planter box which you built out of wood might have eight holes in total every six inches down, but the round pot in which your basil is located could have just one or two holes drilled into the bottom. You want to avoid trying to set rules for regular watering, such as watering each plant every day and instead get to know the things you want to plant and verify whether they need a lot of water and what condition their soil is at any given point. You might decide to water the plants in your home or your outdoor small space only to find that the basil is doing just fine and still has moist soil but your thyme is quite dry on top and drooping. Choosing to water things based on when they need it is best.

Some plants need water twice per day, while others do not. There are a few factors which influence this.

For example...

The size of your container will influence the regularity with which plants must be watered.

The temperature outside will influence it as well. If it is particularly hot one day versus raining another, you might need to increase or decrease the amount you water.

The sunlight can dictate how dry your plants get. If it is quite sunny, your fruits and vegetables may need more water than normal.

The humidity can impact dryness in the soil and how much water the roots of your plants absorb.

The plant itself may have very different requirements. Peppers, for example, require less water than tomatoes or beans.

So how can you tell when your plants need water?

That is simple. Stick your finger into the soil up to the first knuckle. If the soil is wet, you can skip that round of watering. If the soil is dry all the way up to your first knuckle, it needs water.

If you give your fruits and vegetables too much water, they will drown. If you give them too little they will dry out.

It is for this reason that watering your plants is imperative. You need to make sure no excess moisture remains in your container before you give your foods new water. If the soil becomes soggy, it will stunt the growth of your plants and lead to decay.

If possible, you want to water your fruits and vegetables in the morning so that the water does not evaporate under the sunlight immediately. You also want the plants to be dry before the cold evening air sets in. By watering in the morning, you can prevent harmful fungus from accumulating.

When you are adding water, add it slowly until the water begins to drip out of the bottom holes. If you can, use a nozzle or watering can with the multiple holes in lieu of a single stream so that it softly covers the whole of the plant rather than fiercely piercing the soil and harming the roots.

Remember too that small containers dry out faster than large ones, so gauge the water levels accordingly. That said, small seedlings or newly planted seeds require less watering than larger plants in part because of the specific seedling soil designed for improved water retention.

If you are overly cautious and fearful of water loss because of evaporation, you can mulch your fruits and vegetables using dry grass, organic compost, or small pebbles.

Soil Quality

Good soil is essential for good fruits and vegetables no matter the location of your small garden. When you are growing vegetables in containers it is even more important that you have soil which drains well and is aerated. You need soil which can simultaneously retain large amounts of moisture for extended periods of time.

Gardening your fruits and vegetables in containers means you need special soil. You cannot simply take the soil from your backyard and put it in a container. The results will not be everything you are expecting because it will interfere with aeration, moisture retention, and drainage. Garden soil holds water but this can be a problem for container gardening as it could result in too much moisture retention and drowned roots. Another problem with garden soil is that taking soil directly from your yard (or the park across the street) can contain insects, weeds, or diseases which harm your foods.

This is not to say it is impossible. You can absolutely do this, but again, the turnout will not be all that you are expecting. Because of the different conditions, it is best that you make a unique mixture for the soil you use in containers of any kind. If you choose to take some soil from your existing yard, make sure you mix one part builder sand or one part perlite. Never, ever use beach sand in the garden.

Lightweight and porous mixtures will improve water content quality and drainage systems for your containers. In fact, the best

133

soil mixture is one which remains loose, allows water to drain, adds nutrition to the roots, and retains moisture. If you are using commercial soil mixtures, be sure to check if it has chemical additives. If so, stay away. Rely on organic fertilizers like compost, fish weed emulsions, earthworm castings, or garden fertilizers.

The container soil you use must be modified in such a way that it does not negatively impact the moisture retention, drainage, or aeration system. Some container soil is called artificial soil or altered soil because of its mixture of peat, coir fibre, and vermiculite. The mixture you decide to use is really contingent upon the type of foods you want to grow Herbs, for example, will grow better in soils which do not retain excess water for long periods of time. So if you want to grow herbs in your garden you should select a soil mixture with bark, sand, or perlite. But if you want more tropical fruits and vegetables, you need something which holds moisture all day long which is where peat and other less coarse materials are better suited.

Never place the soil mixture directly into the containers. Instead, moisten the mixture before you use it and pour it into a flat tray where it can be sprinkled gently with water. Then mix the content around in such a way that you fluff it a bit. Modified soil will reduce your chances of disease or insects, which is another benefit.

If you wish to make your own mixture you can:

- Mix one quarter garden soil with three-quarters compost or
- Mix one quarter garden soil with one-quarter soilless mixture and half mature compost or
- Mix one quarter garden soil with three-quarters soilless mixture or
- Mix half garden soil with half soilless mixture

Selecting Your Seeds

When you start out cultivating your small space garden, regardless of whether you are using planter boxes or small containers, you can either buy seeds from a local gardening store or produce seeds yourself from your first crops.

If you choose to purchase seeds from a local store you want to first decide on the plants that you wish to cultivate. Think about the fruits and vegetables that you often eat. Consider the time it takes for the fruits or vegetables to manifest. Raspberries, for example, which can be trained to wind up a vertical garden, take two years of gardening before they will bear fruit. Once you have your preliminary list of things, it is important to check on when they should be planted. If you are getting seeds for carrots, you cannot plant them in the early spring. But if you have strawberries on your list of things you want to grow, you can start those in early spring. You will need to create a sort of schedule for your planting.

Find out first what items you want to grow which are perennial, which mean they live for more than two years. Strawberries, for example, are perennials, so you might decide to grow them from seed and leave them in their containers year after year. Other perennials include ginger, oregano, sage, basil, rosemary, tomatoes, sweet potatoes, potatoes, kale, rhubarb, leek, watercress, and peppermint. So items like these can be left in their containers all year round.

But items which are seasonal you might want to rotate out throughout the year. You might, for example, start planting some peppers and when those are all consumed, replacing those peppers with carrots. Knowing the planting dates of the fruits and vegetables you enjoy consuming, and deciding which plants you

135

want to go in containers as perennial and which will be rotated will help you buy seeds accordingly. Of course, you might just want to save yourself the time and buy all of the seeds you want at once.

That being said, when you are buying seeds, ask if the seeds mature early or late and whether they result in large or small plants. You might want to know ahead of time if the seeds you are buying for your small bathroom container will manifest into something large and unruly.

Look for seeds with detailed information printed on the package. Reliable seeds will tell you when you can start germinating the foods indoors, when to plant them in containers, when to plant them in the ground, when you should expect blooms, what size they will become, what water and sun exposure they need, how far apart to plant each seed, etc.... If the container lacks this information, try another variety. Never purchase seeds without adequate information.

If you are buying from a store and some of the seed packets seem faded or have been damaged, avoid these. They might have been placed in an area with too much sun exposure which could damage them. Avoid any expired seeds. If possible, search for non-GMO and organic local seeds. These are the healthiest for any small space garden.

If you want to source seeds yourself from an existing crop, you can save yourself a great deal of hassle with regard to finding the perfect seed all over again. That being said, you want to only source from the best performing crops. If you have dried fruits or slightly rotten fruits, avoid these seeds; they will only be unhealthy and rotten too. Use seeds from the brightest and largest of fruits and vegetables. If you see the seeds are cracked or broken, avoid them. If your fruit is not full mature, do not use the seeds.

Once you source your seeds, you need to store them properly as well. Store them far from the reach of pets or children. If they come into contact with pets at all, as some contain chemicals which could be harmful if digested raw. Store your seeds in an airtight container far from food. You want the seeds to avoid contact with the food in your home. If you want to put your seeds in the refrigerator, you should take them out at least 24 hours before you put them in the soil. They need to reach room temperature before they go in a container. Always wash your hands before you handle seeds, and after.

Germinating at Home

If you want to germinate your plants in your home from seed, you can absolutely do this with just one step of transplanting in the middle. To germinate seeds simply means to grow them from a seed into a seedling, or small baby plant. When you do this, you are better off growing all of the seeds in small containers and then transplanting them into larger containers once they have started to outgrow the small containers. The reason for this is that not all seeds fair well if the seed is placed in a large container.

To do this, you need to create the right environment in your home. There are many small germinating boxes you can order which are plugged into an outlet and then provide warmth for the seeds from the bottom of the try. For these, you can set the tray up in a window sill or anywhere near an outlet and simply use the pre-supplied containers to create miniature greenhouses for each plant. With seedling soil (soil designed to hold more moisture and provide more nutrients) you can place your seeds in the small containers and then secure the tops. Many of the lids have venting locations which you can open and close to allow for air circulation.

The same as any other container for germination, you want to sterilize even those which come with your germination kit. You can do this by first washing the containers out to remove any excess debris or dirt. Then fill a bucket or container large enough to hold the containers for your plants with one part bleach to ten parts water. Leave the containers in there for 30 minutes. After 30 minutes, wash each container out with soap and water. Allow them to air dry.

When you first germinate the seeds you want to keep the lids sealed so that it creates a greenhouse inside, but if you notice that too much moisture is there and the soil is beginning to grow green on top, vent it a bit. You should start to see the small seedlings bursting through the soil in a matter of days.

It is best to place half a dozen seeds in one container and then pick out the strongest ones for transplant.

Alternatively, you can use special grow lights over your germinating seeds to help them grow strong. These generally have pink and blue lights that make your home look like a disco, and the plants need exposure to the lights for roughly 12 hours per day. One color stunts growth, which prevents the plants from getting too leggy—another way of saying that they grow up too tall without the strong base or roots to support the height, and the other keeps them growing strong roots. If you choose to germinate under these lights you can fill one seed per small germinating container and then pick the strongest to transplant, or use bigger containers and place multiple seeds in one container, allocating a single container for a single fruit, herb, or vegetable.

If you are germinating things like cucumbers, tomatoes, or peppers, they require very little soil at the beginning. A fun trick is to simply add a layer of soil as the plant begins to grow. The key here is to watch the plant and look for small stems branching out from the sides of the plant. If you see that the seedlings has its group of four leaf clusters on top and is beginning to form a few legs beneath that, add more soil delicately until those other legs are covered. This will convert the other legs into additional strong roots and force the plant to grow a stronger base while continuing to sprout upward.

Transplant simply means moving the plant from one container to another (or into the ground in your small home garden). For this process, you should treat your young plants delicately. Prepare the new containers by sterilizing them and filling them part way with soil. Then delicately remove the plant, being careful not to disturb the roots, and place it into the middle of the container. Fill the plant up with soil as much as is necessary.

What to Plant

Plants which have compact growth will thrive in containers. Container plants can be transplanted as a plant from one container to a different one. You can also plant seeds in different containers. You should, as mentioned, have an idea of what fruits and vegetables you need to plant so that you can buy pots or containers which are appropriately suited to their size and needs.

You can grow vegetables, herbs, and fruits in containers. Select the plants you want based on the amount of sun the areas where you plan on having your containers receives, as well as the climate where you live, and the foods you want to consume.

You can combine edible flowers, for example, with vegetables and herbs to add a pinch of color and unique salads to your life. You can pick one container garden for one season, then replace it with another plan the next year. You can keep all perennials and avoid having to replace your plants the next year. It is up to you.

Determining what you want to grow is a difficult decision, especially when you start to see how many options are out there. You might love basil and decide on planting that in your home. But then you see that there is the traditional sweet green basil you have come to know and love, as well as a delicious dark purple plant referred to as red basil, and even lemon basil, lime basil, cinnamon basil, spicy bush basil, and sweet Thai basil, among others. Now you have to decide which ones you want.

That being said, depending on where you live and the availability of sunlight, you might have such a decision made for you. Look into the conditions where you live and compare them to the conditions required by the fruits and vegetables you want to plant. It is important to decide where you will place your containers so as to determine how much sunlight is available, and by extension, what you can plant.

You might choose the small pathway alongside your house as your small garden plot, or your balcony, a small rooftop, a wall inside or outside of your home, a windowsill, your frontyard, your backyard, or inside of your home.

Each location will receive a different amount of sun during different times of the day. Once you know the location where you will start your small space garden, you can figure out how many hours of sun it receives.

Full Sun (FS) is a category of sunlight which means six hours of direct sun each day. Partial Sun is another category which refers to less than five hours of direct sunlight each day. Partial Shade (PS) is where your area receives between two and four hours of sunlight. Shade constitutes an area where you receive less than 1 hour of direct sunlight each day.

With that in mind, you need to determine what sunlight your small garden space receives and what you can plant.

Vegetables, especially squash, eggplant, tomatoes, and peppers, all require full sun. Leaf vegetables and root vegetables like kale, peas, beets, carrots, and lettuce require roughly six hours of sunlight. Sage can handle just about six hours of sun. No vegetable can handle complete shade, but a few can handle partial shade like broccoli, beans, spinach, collards, and radishes.

Obviously growing native plants will work out better for you based on your climate. That being said, below is a list of fruits and vegetables which require full sun versus partial sun:

Full Sun (FS)

- Beans
- Carrots
- Corn
- Potatoes
- Sweet potatoes
- Beets
- Grains
- Peas
- Radishes
- Hibiscus
- Spinach
- Cucumbers
- Eggplant
- Squash
- Bell pepper
- Tomatoes

Full Sun/or Partial Sun (PS)

- Kale
- Broccoli
- Cabbage
- Okra
- Cauliflower

- Brussels Sprouts
- Celery

Partial Sun (PS)

- Pepper
- Turnips
- Collards
- Lettuce
- Mustard greens

Combining Foods

You might want to combine certain fruits or vegetables in the same container. This is perfect if you have a large enough container. Pick items which can fit comfortably together. Some items like mint will take over a container and leech the nutrients from other plants sharing the same space, in addition to extending the roots across the entire network of the container. These plants are not fit for sharing. But most are so long as they meet the same sunlight requirements and have roughly the same size and proportion of space.

If you are attempting to combine multiple plants in a single space, you want to make sure they meet the same watering and soil mixtures too. Plants which are acclimated to hot climates will generally have hairy, thick leaves which allow them to retain moisture, but the roots of these plants will dry out in between each watering session. If you put these with plants accustomed to colder temperatures, these plants will require more watering. You might rot the roots of the first set of plants because of the regular watering for the second set.

Soil an also interfere with plans to combine foods. Some foods need soil with better water retention while others do not. Also, consider that different foods have different growing periods. This can work in your favor or not. If you start off cilantro in one container shared with kale, the cilantro might bloom long before the kale is ripe for picking, which might afford your cilantro more room to grow initially and then the kale more room to flourish once the cilantro has been consumed. But if they are both large, bushy plants, like thyme or rosemary, and you plant them at the same time in a shared container, they might fight for space. This can be quite a mess to untangle if you just want to snip a bit of thyme for dinner.

Herbs and Vegetables

Growing your own fruits and vegetables in an urban environment does a bit of additional work compared to only growing flowers. Vegetable gardens are particularly well suited for containers because you can simply move the containers indoors or under cover if the weather becomes too severe in either direction, thus avoiding the loss of or damage to your crops.

The best vegetables for a small garden space in containers is that of dwarf types. Dwarf types of regular vegetables are designed to grow in a small space over a longer period of time. As listed above, many vegetables require full sun exposure, especially fruit-bearing vegetables. Leafy vegetables generally can handle mostly full exposure but some partial exposure. Root vegetables can make sure with partial exposure.

As mentioned above, it is good to know about annuals versus biennials versus perennials. Annuals are plants which you can replant each year like herbs and vegetables. Biennials are those plants which spend the first half of the year growing their roots and their foliage, only to offer seeds and fruits or vegetables in the second half of the year. Perennials, as mentioned, come back year after year like shallots and asparagus. For your garden to be lush and bountiful all year round you will want to choose some summer annuals which will produce blooms during the summer and a range of foliage for the rest of the year. Sage is one great example of this. You can also use small shrubs or ferns to keep things looking lush even when your fruits and vegetables are not in bloom.

Herbs, except for mint, will take a while to grow at first. Of course, mint will take over everything if given the chance, as mentioned.

Your garden plan must meet your dining needs and your environmental conditions. You can move your containers from one area to another to help with the environmental conditions in which you live, and you can make great arrangements with delicious foods without having expertise in the field of gardening.

If you want to set up your small space garden so that it is a welcoming site in your front yard or in the front window sills, you should include bright flowers and try to find flowers or plants which do not need a great deal of water. Nemesia is an ideal plant for this location as it will bring with it a nice scent and beautiful colors. When you are creating your garden you want to make sure that any centerpieces you place in containers are beautiful and low maintenance. Small cups in any color you want can be combined in the center of a table to produce a masterful centerpiece. Succulents such as jade plants are great for a wooden table.

If you are growing your fruits and vegetables in containers of any kind, you need to be cognizant of those which grow upward. Cucumbers, tomatoes, and beans are examples of vine items which might be best reserved for trellises. That being said, you can get away with putting them in any container you wish by adding small trellises to the back off the containers, or using the plastic circular attachments with a single stick to which the main stalk is attached and around which all branches are wound. By having such fixtures as part of your pots, you can wind the plant branches as they grow so that they naturally move upward with growth. This will keep your vine based items healthy and strong.

Herb Garden Designs

We won't go into this much since a great deal of the information you need to set up your herb garden has been covered in the previous chapters. However, if you are planting outdoors, be sure to find a sunny spot with good drainage. Even if you have a shaded yard, you can plant the herbs in containers and shift them around your yard to chase the sun. Choose the herbs you plant based on your interests. If you cook a lot of Asian and Mexican foods, for example, you might want to plant Thai basil, a great deal of cilantro, fresh peppers dotted throughout, and mint. If you enjoy cooking Italian food, don't forget to include parsley, sage, oregano, thyme, and red basil. If you just want it to smell great, plant lots of mint including peppermint and spearmint, and then add some lavender. If you like the all-natural method of home remedies for ailments, plant old-fashioned medicinal herbs like comfrey, lemon balm, aloe, and chamomile. Different herbs can aid different ailments especially when you dry them out and make tea.

VERTICAL CONTAINER

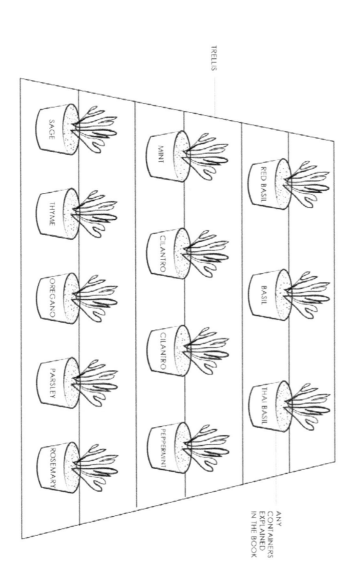

TRELLIS

SAGE THYME OREGANO PARSLEY ROSEMARY

MINT CILANTRO CILANTRO PEPPERMINT

RED BASIL BASIL THAI BASIL

ANY
CONTAINERS
EXPLAINED
IN THE BOOK

147

Conclusion

Today gardens have transformed beyond a simple spacious lawn with rows of flowers adorning the backyard. Gardens have become so much more than a space for weeds thanks to the cultivation of all of these different gardening schemes. Such development now affords homeowners and renters alike the freedom to cultivate gardens in spaces of any size. People living in harsh environments are not forced to go without.

Gardening brings with it multiple benefits, and gardening in a small space is no different. By taking advantage of gardening you can improve your overall health. Regardless of the size of your garden, growing your own food requires you to move about regularly which offers exposure to sunlight and fresh air as well as mild exercise. By growing your own food you and your loved ones benefit from producing organic food free from chemical contaminants. These foods are significantly healthier compared to those foods would you buy at a regular grocery store.

When you take advantage of small spaces you are no longer constrained because of a small terrace or small balcony. You can cultivate natural foods, free from contaminants in any space by using containers to fit the size constraints or relying upon vertical gardening for a terrace. By making use of small spaces you can generate the exact quantities you want when you want them. May this book help you along the way to finding the best garden design to fit your personal taste.

One Last Thing

If you enjoyed this book, you can help me tremendously by leaving a review on Amazon. You have no idea how much this would help.

I also want to give you a chance to win a **$200.00 Amazon Gift card** as a thank-you for reading this book.

All I ask is that you give me some feedback. You can also copy/paste your *Amazon* or *Goodreads review* and this will also count.

Your opinion is super valuable to me. It will only take a minute of your time to let me know what you like and what you didn't like about this book. The hardest part is deciding how to spend the two hundred dollars! Just follow this link.

http://booksfor.review/gardenlayouts

Made in the USA
Las Vegas, NV
06 December 2021

36260756R00090